The
Web Wizard's
Guide to

PHP

THE
WEB WIZARD'S
GUIDE TO
PHP

DAVID A. LASH

Addison
Wesley

Boston San Francisco New York
London Toronto Sydney Tokyo Singapore Madrid
Mexico City Munich Paris Cape Town Hong Kong Montreal

Executive Editor: *Susan Hartman Sullivan*
Project Editor: *Emily Genaway*
Associate Managing Editor: *Pat Mahtani*
Executive Marketing Manager: *Michael Hirsch*
Production Supervision: *Kathy Smith*
Cover and Interior Designer: *Leslie Haimes*
Composition: *Gillian Hall, The Aardvark Group*
Copyeditor: *Chrysta Meadowbrooke*
Proofreader: *Holly McLean-Aldis*
Cover Design: *Gina Hagen Kolenda*
Prepress and Manufacturing: *Caroline Fell*

Access the latest information about Addison-Wesley titles from our World Wide Web site: *http://www.aw.com/cs*

Library of Congress Cataloging-in-Publication Data
Lash, David A.
    The Web wizard's guide to PHP / David A. Lash
        p. cm.
    ISBN 0-321-12174-0
    1. Web site development. 2. PHP (Computer program language) 3. Application Software--Development. 4. Internet programming. I. Title

    TK5105.888 .L384 2003
    005.2′76—dc21   2002074648

12345678910—QWT—040302

TABLE OF CONTENTS

PREFACE

About Addison-Wesley's Web Wizard Series

The beauty of the Web is that, with a little effort, anyone can harness its power to create sophisticated Web sites. *Addison-Wesley's Web Wizard Series* helps readers master the Web by presenting a concise introduction to one important Internet topic or technology in each book. The books start from square one and assume no prior experience with the technology being covered. Mastering the Web doesn't come with a wave of a magic wand, but by studying these accessible, highly visual textbooks, readers will be well on their way.

The series is written by instructors familiar with the challenges beginners face when first learning the material. To this end, the Web Wizard books offer more than a cookbook approach: they emphasize principles and offer clear explanations, giving the reader a strong foundation of knowledge on which to build.

Numerous features highlight important points and aid in learning:

☆ Tips—important points to keep in mind

☆ Shortcuts—time-saving ideas

☆ Warnings—things to watch out for

☆ Review questions and hands-on exercises

☆ On-line references—Web sites to visit for more information

Supplements

Supplementary materials for the books, including updates, additional examples, and source code are available at `http://www.aw.com/webwizard`. Also available for instructors adopting a book from the series are instructors' manuals, test banks, PowerPoint slides, solutions, and Course Compass—a dynamic online course management system powered by Blackboard. Please contact your sales representative for the instructor resources access code.

About This Book

This book is an introduction to using PHP to develop Web applications. No previous programming experience is required, although prior experience working with HTML is helpful. The book strives to be a visual learning tool for students and developers. It uses dozens of diagrams to illustrate different PHP statement syntax. Also, the book employs many short script segments to provide concrete examples of how things work. Finally, since people often want to know why they need to learn something, the book uses several short Web application examples (15–25 lines long) with browser output and line-by-line descriptions. These Web application examples show useful applications such as a Web survey, hit counter, sales event countdown, revenue calculator, form verification, product order entry, inventory management, remembering user preference, and guest books.

The book also contains a wealth of end of chapter review material with many questions and hands-on assignments derived from actual classroom assignments and projects. Since skill levels can vary greatly, many hands-on exercises have optional portions that vary in level of difficulty. If you are reading this book without taking a class, try one or two hands-on exercises in each chapter to apply the material. Like learning to ride a bike, the best way to learn a new language is to practice.

Acknowledgments

This book was a team effort by the many people who helped create it. I owe thanks to Susan Hartman-Sullivan and Emily Genaway for having faith in me in the first place and providing tremendous support to keep this project moving. Also thanks to Kathy Smith who did an excellent job coordinating the final stages of this project. I owe special thanks to Chrysta Meadowbrooke for her excellent work in copyediting this material and to Gillian Hall for her wonderful typesetting. In addition, the book reviewers offered many great ideas and comments that truly made this a better book. These reviewers include

Pete J. Aleman: Community College of Southern Nevada

Molly Pickral Cadieux: University of Virginia

Dr. Cynthia L. Corrite: Creighton University

Andy Deck: Artcode.org

Daniel Dementiev: Marshall University

Rod Ford: Tulane University

Todd A. Gibson: University of Colorado at Denver

Steve Hodges: Cabrillo College

Carl G. Looney: University of Nevada

I especially want to express my gratitude to my wife, Denise, and sons (Christopher, Matthew, and Bryant) for supporting me at home throughout this project. Thanks, guys for your encouragement, support, and patience. (We can now go on a summer vacation in peace.) Finally I owe the greatest gratitude to God for giving me the talent and patience to write this book.

David A. Lash
June 2002

The Web Wizard's Guide to PHP

CHAPTER ONE

INTRODUCTION TO PHP

I f you have not heard of PHP before, it may sound like some sort of chemical process or the latest weight-loss supplement. Actually, PHP is a programming language used to extend the capabilities of Hypertext Markup Language (HTML) documents and create dynamic Web applications. In this chapter, we will introduce the PHP scripting language and explain some background about the language and how it works. Next, we will describe the software and components you will need to get started, and detail the steps you can use to create and run a simple PHP script. Finally, we will look at PHP's basic syntax and how you can generate HTML from a PHP script.

Chapter Objectives

☆ To understand what PHP is and how a PHP script works with a Web Browser and a Web Server

☆ To learn what software and components you need to get started with PHP

☆ To create and run a simple PHP script

☆   To generate HTML output from a PHP script

☆   To learn how to include comments in PHP scripts

◎◎ PHP and the Web

Web Technology Background

Before you start learning about developing PHP scripts, let's review some Web technology background. **Web browsers** (for example, Internet Explorer or Netscape) are software programs that understand how to retrieve and display files in various file formats. For example, a Web browser can

☆   Display a text file in HTML format

☆   Display picture files that use Graphics Interchange Format (GIF) or Joint Photographic Experts Group (JPEG) format

☆   Play a sound file in Windows wavform (WAV) audio file format

HTML files are a mixture of text to display and HTML-coded commands. These coded commands, called **HTML tags**, provide instructions to Web browsers about how to display the document's text. For example, an HTML tag might define a hyperlink, the text size, or many other things. Figure 1.1 shows a basic HTML document (top screen) and shows that same HTML file displayed in a Web browser (bottom screen).

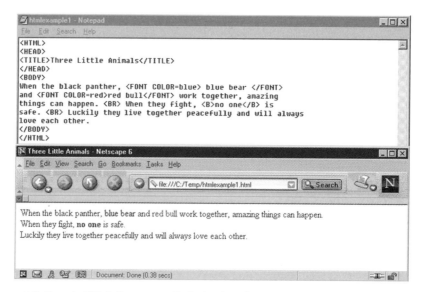

Figure 1.1 Sample HTML Document Code (top) and How It Appears in a Browser Window (bottom)

Using HTML works great for sharing and displaying static documents and images over the Internet. In fact, at first only static documents and images were available on the World Wide Web. Soon it became clear that additional technologies were needed to create dynamic Web applications that could do things like verify forms, react to end-user input, and access databases. Eventually powerful technologies were developed—like CGI/Perl, PHP, and Active Server Pages (among others)—that can enhance HTML documents when they run on a **Web server**. A Web server is a computer that stores files and makes them available over the Internet. Web servers also run special Web server software that helps provide data files, execute application programs, and return results over the Internet.

☆**TIP**   **Different Web Server Software**

Web server software can run on many different types of machines, including Microsoft Windows, UNIX, and Macintosh systems. As of this writing, the Apache software is the most popular Web server software, and it runs on both UNIX and Windows systems. Other Web server programs include Microsoft's Internet Information Server (IIS) for Windows systems and StarNine's WebStar for Macintosh systems.

What Is PHP?

Rasmus Lerdorf created PHP in 1994. He first used it to build extensions into HTML documents to enhance his personal home page. (In fact, PHP was originally called *Personal Home Page*.) As Lerdorf freely distributed the program source, PHP gained popularity and became an Apache Software Foundation project. The Apache Software Foundation is an open source software (OSS) collaborative software development community that provides free software downloads. Eventually, PHP's name was changed to *PHP Hypertext Preprocessor*. Today, according to a Netcraft (http://www.netcraft.com) Web server survey, PHP currently has over 7 million sites that use it and its use is increasing rapidly.

Using PHP to enhance Web pages has several advantages.

☆ *Easy to use:* As previously mentioned, PHP is not a hard language to use and understand even if you have never programmed before. If you are familiar with high-level languages such as Perl, C, or C++, you will particularly find PHP a snap.

☆ *Open source:* Since PHP is developed as an OSS project, it is available for free download over the Internet. Support for OSS projects is available through many online Web pages, electronic bulletin boards, and e-mail lists. Technical questions and new feature requests are often handled much more quickly in the OSS community than they are with software vendors, who might actually have fewer people providing support. Finally, open source means the program source code is available for you to view and change if you really desire.

☆ *Multiple platform:* PHP can be installed on UNIX- and Windows-based machines. This means that it is possible to create applications that can be ported to different environments (for example, between UNIX and Windows machines).

 Language support for databases: PHP supports a variety of different database systems that include MySQL, Informix, Oracle, and Sybase, to name a few. Its interface into these databases is straightforward, easy to use, and quite efficient.

☆TIP   PHP Is Similar to Some Other Languages

If you are familiar with other high-level programming languages such as Perl, C, C++, or Java, you will likely recognize many of the language features in PHP. Perl and C have had particular influence on many of PHP's features, such as regular expressions, file input/output (I/O), and functions. If you are not familiar with these languages, don't worry—PHP is easy to learn.

Accessing PHP-Enhanced HTML Documents

When you access a file with embedded PHP commands, several steps occur that are fairly invisible to the end user. Figure 1.2 shows the sequence of steps when a Web browser requests such a file over the Internet. These steps include the following.

☆ *Enter a Web address to a PHP file.* When a user enters a Web address to a PHP file in a Web browser (for example, `http://www.mypage.com/ funstuff.php`), the request is sent over the Internet and the appropriate Web server receives the request. (See steps 1–3 in Figure 1.2.)

☆ *Process the request on the Web server.* When the Web server examines the request, it finds the requested file and then uses the PHP language environment to execute any PHP commands. It then sends the PHP output back over the Internet (with any HTML tags used still embedded in it). Since the PHP language environment is built directly into the Web server software, this process can be very quick. (See steps 4-6.)

☆ *Receive the file and interpret any HTML in the browser.* When the browser receives the file, it uses any HTML tags to determine how the document should be displayed, and then the browser displays the document. (See step 7.)

◎◎ Getting Started with PHP

You can begin developing PHP scripts without extensive software tools or expensive software licenses. To start developing PHP scripts you need the following:

☆ A Web server with PHP built into it

☆ A client machine with a basic text editor and Internet connection

☆ FTP or Telnet software

Let's discuss each of these items next.

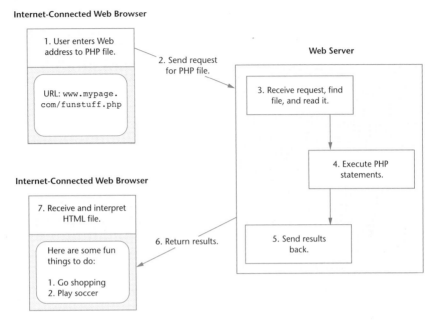

Figure 1.2 Sequence for Accessing and Interpreting PHP Files

A Web Server with Built-in PHP

Although PHP's usage continues to grow, not all Web servers run software with built-in PHP. If you are going to use an external Web server (for example, through an Internet server provider [ISP]), you need to check with the Web server provider to ensure that PHP is supported. If PHP is not already built into the Web server you might suggest the provider obtain PHP for free and install it. (But don't hold your breath; you may need to look for another Web server or ISP.)

You can also install your own Web server software on a machine of your choice and build PHP into that machine (though this can get a little involved and probably is not a good choice for the novice). For example, you can download the Apache Web Server software, add on PHP, and then install the entire package. The Apache Web Server is by far the most widely used Web Server software and it is also available for free (as an OSS project at `http://www.apache.org`). You can install Apache on Windows-based, Linux-based, or UNIX-based machines.

Regardless of whether you use an external Web server or run your own server, you should verify the PHP version that the Web server is running. This book is written for PHP 4.0. If you have an older version of PHP, some of the features described in this book might behave differently or may not work at all. To determine your Web server's version of PHP, ask your Web server administrator or use the built-in `phpinfo()` function. (A description of how to use `phpinfo()` is given later in this chapter.)

A Client Machine with a Basic Text Editor

You can develop PHP applications on almost any client machine with an Internet connection. For example, you can use a Windows machine, a Macintosh machine, a Linux machine, or a UNIX workstation. On these machines you can use a simple text editor such as Notepad on Windows or pico, vi, or Emacs on UNIX or Linux machines to create your PHP scripts.

FTP or Telnet Software

If you elect to use a Web server external to your client machine (for example, a server provided by your ISP), you need a way to get your PHP scripts onto the Web server. There are at least two different ways to develop PHP scripts with an external Web server. You can use either FTP or Telnet.

☆ *FTP:* You can do your PHP development on your own computer and then use an FTP program to copy your pages to the Web server to run them. Using FTP means that every time you change your script you have to use FTP to copy it back and forth between the computer and the Web server.

☆ *Telnet:* In some cases you can do your PHP development directly on a Web server using Telnet. This way you can connect to a Web server over the Internet and then run commands, create files, and develop software directly on the Web server. Using Telnet to develop your scripts on the Web server means that you need to understand more about navigating and working on the Web server (although the development process is probably faster). Sometimes, because of security concerns, Telnet access is not allowed.

☆**WARNING** Obtaining FTP and Telnet Software

You can find several different FTP and Telnet software programs available on the Internet as freeware and for purchase. However, before obtaining any FTP or Telnet program you should check whether your Web server requires the more secure encrypted versions (such as SSH Telnet or FTP supporting Secure Socket Layer).

◎◎ Exploring the Basic PHP Development Process

Once you have selected a Web server and have an Internet-connected client machine, you are ready to start developing your first PHP application. As you develop PHP scripts you will repeat a set of development steps over and over. The following describes these steps, assuming you are using FTP to copy files to an external Web server. (Appendix A shows how to connect and use Telnet.)

1. Create a PHP script file and save it to a local disk.

2. Use FTP to copy the file to the server.

3. Access your file using a browser.

Each of these steps is reviewed next.

Creating a PHP Script File and Saving It to a Local Disk

As previously described, you can use a number of different editors to create your PHP script files. Figure 1.3 shows a PHP script created in Notepad. Note how the PHP script starts with a `<?php` tag and ends with `?>`. Between these tags is a single PHP `print` statement. Suppose you enter these lines (using your favorite editor on your computer) and save them in a file called `First.php`.

```
First.php - Notepad                                    _ □ ×
File   Edit   Search   Help
<?PHP
  print ("A simple initial script");
?>
```

Figure 1.3 An Initial PHP Script

☆ **TIP**   **Alternative PHP Delimiters**

You can alternatively start your PHP scripts with the `<script>` tag as follows:

```
<script language="PHP">
print ("A simple initial script");
</script>
```

If your PHP installation has `short_open_tag` enabled in its configuration file, you can use `<?` and `?>` as PHP short delimiters. Also, if `asp_tags` is enabled in the PHP configuration file, you can use `<%` and `%>` as delimiters.

☆ **WARNING**   **Be Careful with the File Extension**

Be careful to include the `.php` file extension when you name your PHP files. Often a `.php` file extension is required for PHP scripts to work properly. For example, calling your script `myfile.php` might work correctly, but calling it `myfile.html` might not. (For an Apache Web Server the file extension used is a configuration option.) You may need to check with your ISP or Web server administrator to determine what file extension to use.

Copying a File to a Web Server with FTP

As previously mentioned, you can use FTP to copy files from your computer onto your Web server. If you are using FTP to connect to your Web server, use the following steps to establish an FTP connection and copy your files to your Web server.

1. *Connect to the Internet and start FTP.* If you are not already connected, you need to connect to the Internet. Once connected, start your FTP software.

2. *Connect to your Web server with FTP.* Once the FTP program starts you will receive an initial FTP login screen. You will need to supply your Web server's

host name (for example, webwizard.aw.com), your user ID (for example, phppgm), and your password.

3. *Copy files to the Web server.* Once you establish an FTP connection to your Web server, you will see a screen similar to the one shown in Figure 1.4. Use this screen to copy your files from your computer to your Web server. The files and directories on your computer will appear on the left side of this screen (for example, `First.php`, `-c-`, and `-d-` in Figure 1.4), with the current directory showing in the top box (`C:\PHP` in the figure). Your files and directories on the Web server will appear on the right (for example, `test.html`, `C2`, `C3`, and `test.php` in the figure). To copy a file, first change to the correct current directory on your Web server using the right side of the FTP window (for example, `/home/phppgm/public_html`). Next, highlight the file on your computer on the left side, and then click the right arrow (→) to copy the file to the Web server.

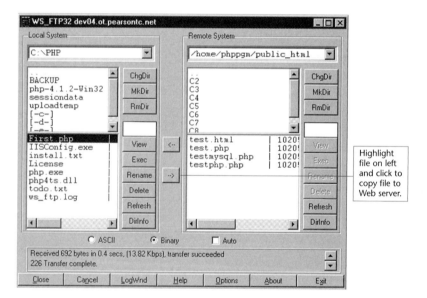

Figure 1.4 A Successful FTP Connection Screen

Accessing Your File Using a Browser

Once you have copied your file to the Web server, you can start your browser and enter the Web address to your file to test your script. Figure 1.5 shows the browser output of the `First.php` script located at `http://webwizard.aw.com/~phppgm/First.php`.

Figure 1.5 The Output of the First.php Script Viewed over the Internet

Dealing with Problems: The Importance of Proper Syntax

Ideally, your PHP scripts will be correct immediately without any errors. In reality, however, there are often problems that need to be corrected. If you have a **syntax error**, you have written one or more PHP statements that are grammatically incorrect in the PHP language. For example, Figure 1.6 points out the syntax of the `print` statement.

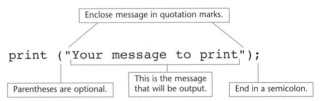

Figure 1.6 The Syntax of a PHP `print` Statement

If you forget a quotation mark or parenthesis, you will receive a syntax error when you access your page. For example, suppose your PHP script looked like the following code. (The line numbers are placed there for reference; do not use them in your scripts.)

```
1. <?php
2.    print ("A simple initial script);
3. ?>
```

In this case, line 2 is missing an ending quotation mark. If you were to place these lines into a file, copy them to your Web server, and access them with a browser, you would receive the output shown in Figure 1.7. Note that even though the syntax error is on line 2 of the script, since PHP cannot match up the quotation marks, it inaccurately reports the error on line 4.

Figure 1.7 Output of a PHP Script with a Syntax Error

If your script does contain syntax errors, don't panic! Instead, realize that when you enter commands with the wrong syntax, PHP can only *guess* what the problem is. Sometimes, the errors indicated by PHP are only clues about what is wrong. For example, if you accidentally put only one quotation mark in a `print` statement, this will confuse PHP since it's not clear where the `print` statement ends. When you have a syntax error, you need to re-edit your script, correct the error, save the script, republish it, and then recheck it. For large scripts, you might have to do this process several times until all the syntax errors are removed.

☆ **SHORTCUT Installing PHP Locally**

If you use FTP to copy files to the Web server, testing script syntax and removing errors can be tedious. You can obtain a Windows version of PHP from `http://www.php.net` and install it on your Windows machine. (Installation is easy; instructions are provided on the Web site.) Then you can test your script's syntax locally before copying the file to the Web server. For example, if you install PHP on your computer in `C:\php`, you can execute a PHP script at `C:\temp\test.php` by entering the following at the MS-DOS prompt:

```
C:\php\php  C:\temp\test.php
```

When you write PHP scripts, it is important to notice and adhere to each statement's required syntax. Using the correct statement syntax the first time can greatly reduce the time required to develop PHP scripts. Throughout the text, we will discuss each specific statement syntax as it is introduced, but the following list highlights some overall PHP syntax issues.

☆ *Be careful to use quotation marks, parentheses, and brackets in pairs.* When writing statements that use starting and ending quotation marks, parentheses, or brackets, be careful to include both. As you saw from the example in Figure 1.7, using only one quotation mark can cause confusing syntax errors.

☆ *Most PHP commands end with a semicolon (;).* Be careful to include the ending semicolon when a statement requires it. Forgetting a required semicolon will generate an error message.

☆ *Be careful of case.* PHP commands are case insensitive, but you should still adopt a consistent case usage. For example, each of the following print statements is valid.

```
Print ("A simple initial script");
print ("A simple initial script");
PRINT ("A simple initial script");
```

If you adopt a consistent case practice for PHP commands (for example, using all lowercase letters), your scripts will be more readable. Also, consistent case usage will be helpful when you later use case-sensitive language constructs (such as variable and function names).

☆ *PHP ignores blank spaces.* PHP lets you freely use blank spaces and lines to improve the readability of your scripts. For example, we could write the print statement we used earlier in either of the following ways and still obtain the same output as that shown in Figure 1.5.

```
print
    ("A simple initial script");

print          (" A simple initial script" );
```

☆TIP   Determining the PHP Version on Your Web Server

You can use the following PHP script to determine the version of PHP your Web server runs. Input this script into a file, publish it on the Internet, and view it with a browser.

```
<?php phpinfo(); ?>
```

The screen output will indicate information about the installed PHP version and the settings on various PHP and Web Server Software configuration options.

◎◎ Embedding PHP Statements within HTML Documents

A common way to use PHP is to embed PHP scripts within HTML tags in an HTML document. When PHP statements are embedded in an HTML document, any output from PHP is used as part of the HTML document. For example, consider the following script. (Figure 1.8 shows its output when viewed in a browser window.)

```
1. <html> <head>
2. <title> Generating HTML From PHP</title></head>
3. <body> <h1> Generating HTML From PHP</h1>
4. <?php
5.     print ("Using PHP has <i>some advantages:</i>");
6.     print ("<ul><li>Speed</li><li>Ease of use</li>
                        <li>Functionality</li></ul>");
7.     print ("</body></html>");
8. ?>
```

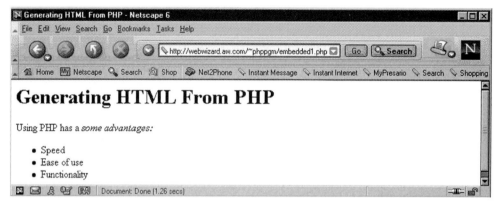

Figure 1.8 Output of a PHP Script Embedded in an HTML Document

Here's an explanation of this script.

☆ Lines 1–3 start the HTML document and create an HTML document title.

☆ Lines 4–5 start the PHP script and then output a line of text that uses the HTML italics tag.

☆ Line 6–8 output an HTML bullet list and line 7 outputs tags to end the HTML document.

☆ **TIP   Using New Line Characters to Improve Source Readability**

You can output a sequence of \n characters in `print` statements to provide line breaks in the HTML source document. The \n characters will not display on the browser but can be used to make the HTML document more readable when you view the HTML source from a Web browser.

☆ **SHORTCUT   Using Backslash (\) to Generate HTML Tags with print()**

Sometimes you want to output an HTML tag that also requires double quotation marks. You can use the backslash ("\") character to signal that the double quotation marks themselves should be output, as in the following example:

```
print ("<font color=\"blue\">");
```

The above statement would output:

```
<font color="blue">
```

◎◎ Using Comments with PHP Scripts

Comments enable you to include descriptive text along with the PHP script. Comment lines are ignored when the script runs; they do not slow down the run-time. Comments have two common uses.

1. *Describe the overall script purpose.* For large scripts, developers often include a couple of beginning comments that indicate who wrote the script, when, and a short overview of the script's task.

2. *Describe particularly tricky script lines.* Comments can also be judiciously placed after particularly tricky script lines to help describe what they do. This use can be invaluable to anyone trying to understand the script.

You can create a comment by preceding the comment text with two forward slashes (//). For example, the following script contains only a comment; therefore it does nothing when run.

```php
<?php
// This is a comment
?>
```

You can also place comments on the same line of a script line. For example, you could write the PHP script shown in Figure 1.3 as follows.

```php
<?php
   print ("A simple initial script");   //Output a line
?>
```

The following example revises the script from Figure 1.8 to include comments. Its output is the same as shown in Figure 1.8.

```
1.   <html> <head>
2.   <title> Generating HTML From PHP</title> </head>
3.   <body> <h1> Generating HTML From PHP</h1>
4.   <?php
5.   //
6.   // Example script to output HTML tags
7.   //
8.   print ("Using PHP has <i>some advantages:</i>");
9.   print ("<ul><li>Speed</li><li>Ease of use</li>
     <li>Functionality</li></ul>"); //Output bullet list
10.  print ("</body></html>");
11.  ?>
```

Here's a brief explanation of this script.

☆ Lines 1–3 are HTML tags that start the HTML document.

☆ Lines 4–7 start the PHP script and output three lines of comments.

☆ Lines 8–10 output the remainder of the HTML document. Note how line 9 includes a comment at the end of the PHP statement.

☆**TIP**   **Alternative Comment Syntax**

PHP allows a couple of additional ways to create comments. One style creates a comment by using a pound sign (#). For example, the following is a valid PHP script with a comment.

```php
<?php
    phpinfo();           # This is a built-in function
?>
```

PHP allows another comment style to provide an easy way to create multiline comments. PHP will assume any lines starting after the /* characters and ending before the */ characters are comments. So, for example, the following is a script with a multiline comment.

```php
<?php
/*
A script that gets information about the
PHP version being used.
*/
    phpinfo();
?>
```

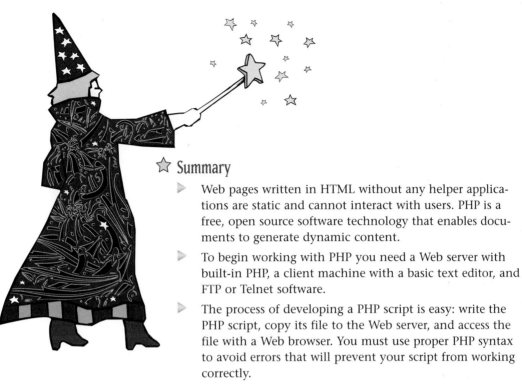

☆ Summary

▷ Web pages written in HTML without any helper applications are static and cannot interact with users. PHP is a free, open source software technology that enables documents to generate dynamic content.

▷ To begin working with PHP you need a Web server with built-in PHP, a client machine with a basic text editor, and FTP or Telnet software.

▷ The process of developing a PHP script is easy: write the PHP script, copy its file to the Web server, and access the file with a Web browser. You must use proper PHP syntax to avoid errors that will prevent your script from working correctly.

▷ You can embed a PHP script within an HTML document or run it as a stand-alone script. The PHP `print` statement lets you output HTML tags and text from HTML documents.

▷ Descriptive comments can be included along with PHP script statements by preceding the comment with two forward slashes (//).

☆ Online References

The principal PHP site that includes manuals, downloads, and answers to frequently asked questions
`http://www.php.net`

A PHP tutorial and overview information
`http://hotwired.lycos.com/webmonkey`

Introductory articles about PHP
`http://www.zend.com/zend/art/intro.php`

Information on the Apache Software Foundation, including its various projects and downloads
`http://www.apache.org`

Usage information and statistics on Web server software
`http://www.netcraft.com`

☆ Review Questions

1. What does the acronym PHP stand for? When was PHP invented?
2. Describe the steps that occur when a Web browser requests a PHP-enhanced Web page.

3. What are three advantages of PHP?

4. What are the differences between FTP and Telnet?

5. What is a Web server? What are two functions that it performs?

6. What are the basic steps to follow each time you develop and run a PHP script?

7. What is a syntax error? What steps do you take to repair and republish a file with a syntax error?

8. What character sequences do you use to start and end PHP scripts?

9. What are script comments? What character sequences do you use to create comments?

10. What PHP command can you use to output HTML commands from a PHP script?

☆ Hands-On Exercises

1. Modify the script from Figure 1.3 and publish it on the Web. Change the print statement to be the following two lines.

```
print ("Steady plodding brings prosperity.\n ");
print ("Hasty speculation leads to poverty.");
```

Notice the addition of the \n characters in the first line. What happens when you view the source from the browser? Try adding another instance of \n in the first line, as shown below.

```
print ("Steady plodding brings prosperity.\n\n ");
print ("Hasty speculation leads to poverty.");
```

View the source again from the browser. What was the difference?

2. Input the following PHP script and view it over the Internet. What version of PHP are you running?

```
<?php phpinfo(); ?>
```

Optional: Carefully look at the phpinfo() output. Can you tell what Web server software is installed?

3. Modify the script from Figure 1.3 to add comments at the beginning that indicate your name, the date you are creating the script, and a one-line description of the script. Publish your file and view it over the Internet.

4. The following script has some syntax errors in it. Input this script into a file, correct the syntax errors, and get it to correctly display over the Internet.

```
<html><head>
<title> A Very Troubled Web Page </title></head>
<body>
<?php
```

```
        Prints ("<h1> Welcome to My Web Site </h1>")
        Prints ("<br> <font color="blue"> This page is
            being")
        Prints ("generated by PHP")
        Prints <br> but be careful there are errors)
    ?>
    </body></html>
```

5. Create a PHP script that outputs the following HTML document. Save your script on your Web server and view it over the Internet. Generate all the HTML tags within the <body> tag using PHP.

```
<html> <head> <title> More on PHP </title></head>
<body bgcolor="blue">
<h1> More on PHP </h1>
If you have ever used programming languages such as
<i>Perl, C, or C++ </i>, many of the features of
PHP will be familiar. <br><br>In particular, you
might notice some similarity to Perl with features
such as
    <ul>
    <li> Regular expressions  </li>
    <li> Associative arrays </li>
    <li> File I/O </li>
    </ul>
</body></html>
```

CHAPTER TWO

USING VARIABLES

N ow that we have discussed some PHP background information and learned how to create and publish basic PHP scripts, let's explore how to use PHP variables. We will discuss how to define variable names, set variable values, and use some basic variable operators. Since PHP variables can receive input values from HTML forms, we'll also review how to create and use HTML form elements (such as checklists, radio boxes, text boxes, and submit buttons) and then see how to use them to pass data to PHP scripts.

Chapter Objectives

- ☆ To learn how to store and access data in PHP variables
- ☆ To understand how to create and manipulate numeric and string variables
- ☆ To review how to create HTML input forms
- ☆ To learn how to pass data from HTML forms to PHP scripts

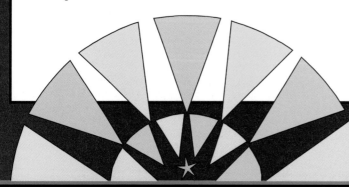

◎◎ Using PHP Variables

Variables are used to store and access data in computer memory. A **variable name** is a label used within a script to refer to the data. You can assign a data value to the variable name, change that value, print it out, and perform many different operations (for example, multiplication, addition). In PHP, variables can hold numeric data (for example, 1, 1239.12, –123), character string data (for example, "Extra Large", "John Smith", "Rhode Island"), or even entire *lists* of numeric or string data called arrays. Let's concentrate on numeric and character string variables now; we will cover arrays in Chapter Five.

In your PHP scripts, you can create and use your own variables by assigning a value to a variable name. Simply place the variable's name on the left side of an equal sign (=) and the value on the right side of the equal sign. That value will then be stored or saved into computer memory. The PHP statements shown in Figure 2.1 use two variables: `$cost` and `$months`.

```
Name of variable          $cost = 4.25;       Variable's new value
                          $months = 12;
```

Figure 2.1 Assigning Values to Variables

Note that each PHP statement ends with a semicolon (;). Also note that the first statement assigns the value 4.25 to the variable `$cost` and the second statement assigns the value 12 to the variable `$months`. These assignments represent the current values of `$cost` and `$months`. You can also assign new values to variables. For example, consider the following PHP statements.

```
$days = 3;
$newdays = 100;
$days = $newdays;
```

This example uses two variables (`$days` and `$newdays`). At the end of these three lines, `$days` and `$newdays` both have values of 100.

You can select just about any set of characters for a variable name in PHP, as long as you adhere to the following rules.

☆ The first character must be a dollar sign ($).

☆ The second character must be a letter or an underscore character (_).

> ☆ **TIP**   **Choose Descriptive Variable Names**
>
> It is good programming style to select variable names that help describe their function. For example, `$counter` is more descriptive than `$c` or `$ctr`, and `$dollars` is more descriptive than `$dol` or `$dlr`. The idea is to write self-documenting statements that other people will easily understand.

Thus `$baseball`, `$_time`, `$X`, `$Numb_of_bricks`, `$num_houses`, and `$counter1` are all valid PHP variable names. Conversely, `$123go`, `$1counter`, and `counter` are not valid choices.

☆ **WARNING** Variable Names Are Case Sensitive

PHP variable names are case sensitive, so be careful about how you use upper- and lowercase letters in variable names. For example, $numTimes, $Numtimes, and $NumTimes are all different variable names.

Combining Variables and the print Statement

In the first chapter, we used a `print` statement to output HTML tags and text. You can also use a `print` statement to output a variable's value by placing the variable name inside the double quotes of the `print` statement. That is, to print out the value of `$x`, write the following PHP statement:

```
print ("$x");
```

You can also include text to output using the `print` statement. The following code will output "Bryant is 6 years old".

```
$age=6;
print ("Bryant is $age years old.");
```

Consider the following sample PHP script and its browser output in Figure 2.2, which shows how to initialize variables (lines 5–6) and output their values (line 10). (Do not enter the numbers at the start of each line.)

```
1.  <html>
2.  <head> <title>Variable Example </title> </head>
3.  <body>
4.  <?php
5.      $first_num  = 12;
6.      $second_num = 356;
7.      $temp = $first_num;          ──────  $temp is assigned 12.
8.      $first_num = $second_num;    ──────  $first_num is assigned 356.
9.      $second_num  = $temp;        ──────  $second_num is assigned 12.
10.     print ("first_num= $first_num <br>
               second_num=$second_num");
11. ?> </body> </html>
```

Figure 2.2 Output of a Script That Switches the Values of Two Variables

Here's a brief explanation of the script.

★ Lines 1–3 start the HTML document.

★ Lines 4–6 begin the PHP script, assigning the value 12 to $first_num and the value 356 to $second_num.

★ Line 7 assigns the value 12 to the variable $temp.

★ Lines 8–9 assign the values 356 to $first_num and then 12 to $second_num.

★ Line 10 outputs the values of $first_num and $second_num.

★ Line 11 first ends the PHP script and then the HTML document.

Using Arithmetic Operators

Using arithmetic operators, you can create expressions to manipulate variable data values. To do so, use **operators** such as a plus sign (+) for addition and a minus sign (–) for subtraction. For example, consider the following PHP statements.

```
<?php
   $apples = 12;
   $oranges = 14;
   $total_fruit = $apples + $oranges;
   print ("The total number of fruit is $total_fruit");
?>
```

These PHP statements would output "The total number of fruit is 26."

Addition and subtraction are just two numeric operations that PHP supports. Table 2.1 lists the PHP common numeric operators and gives an example of each operator's use.

Table 2.1 Common PHP Numeric Operators

Operator	Effect	Example	Result
+	Addition	$x = 2 + 2;	$x is assigned 4.
–	Subtraction	$y = 3; $y = $y - 1;	$y is assigned 2.
/	Division	$y = 14 / 2;	$y is assigned 7.
*	Multiplication	$z = 4; $y = $z * 4;	$y is assigned 16.
%	Remainder	$y = 14 % 3;	$y is assigned 2.

The following example illustrates an HTML document with a PHP script that uses numeric operators. It calculates the total possible revenue and profit for a hypothetical theater assuming it has 12 rows with 20 seats in each row. The theater also charges $3.75 per ticket and has a fixed building cost of $300. Figure 2.3 shows the script's output.

```
1.   <html>
2.   <head> <title>Variable Example </title> </head>
3.   <body>
4.   <?php
5.       $columns = 20;
6.       $rows = 12;
7.       $total_seats = $rows * $columns;
8.
9.       $ticket_cost = 3.75;
10.      $total_revenue = $total_seats * $ticket_cost;
11.
12.      $building_cost = 300;
13.      $profit = $total_revenue - $building_cost;
14.
15.      print ("Total Seats are $total_seats <br>");
16.      print ("Total Revenue is $total_revenue <br>");
17.      print ("Total Profit is $profit");
18. ?> </body> </html>
```

Annotations:
- Assign 240 to $total_seats. (line 7)
- Assign 900 (240 * 3.75) to $total_revenue. (line 10)
- Assign 600 to $profit (900–300). (line 13)

Figure 2.3 Output of a Script Using Numeric Operators

Let's briefly examine this script.

☆ Lines 1–3 start the HTML document.

☆ Lines 4–7 start the PHP script, assigning the values 20 to $columns, 12 to $rows, and then 240 to $total_seats.

☆ Lines 9–10 assign the values 3.75 to $ticket_cost and 900 to $total_revenue (240 * 3.75).

☆ Lines 12–13 assign the values 300 to $building_cost and 600 to $profit (900 – 300).

☆ Lines 15–17 output the values of $total_seats, $total_revenue, and $profit.

☆ Line 18 first ends the PHP script and then the HTML document.

⭐ **WARNING Using Variables with Undefined Values**

PHP will not generate an error if you accidentally use a variable that does not have a value assigned to it. Instead, the variable will have no value (called a **null value**). When a variable with a null value is used in an expression PHP, PHP may *not* generate an error and may complete the expression evaluation. For example, the following PHP script will not generate an error when viewed over the Internet with a browser.

```
<?php
  $y = 3;
  $y=$y + $x + 1;        // $x has a null value
  print ("x=$x y=$y");
?>
```

The above script would output "x= y=4".

⭐ **SHORTCUT Automatic Increment/Decrement Operators**

Since it is common for scripts to increment or decrement a variable's value by 1 (for example, to decrement an inventory count), PHP supports two additional operators that automatically do this. If you precede a variable with ++ or -- PHP will automatically add or subtract 1 to the variable. For example, the following script would output "x=1 and now y=1".

```
<?php
  $x=0;  $y=2;
  print "x=";
  print ++$x;
  --$y;
  print " and now y=$y";
?>
```

Writing Complex Expressions

You can include multiple operators in a statement to create complex expressions. When using multiple operators, you need to be aware of the **operator precedence rules** that define the order in which the operators are evaluated. For example, consider the following expression:

```
$x = 5 + 2 * 6;
```

The value of $x is either 42 or 17, depending on whether you evaluate the addition or the multiplication first. Because PHP evaluates multiplication operations before addition operations, this expression evaluates to 17. PHP follows the precedence rules listed below.

☆ First it evaluates operators within parentheses.

☆ Next it evaluates multiplication and division operators.

☆ Finally it evaluates addition and subtraction operators.

To see how these precedence rules work, consider the PHP statements shown below. The first two equations are equivalent, and both evaluate to 80. The first statement uses the precedence rules given above, and the second clarifies these rules by using parentheses. The third statement uses parentheses to set a different order for operator evaluation, and it evaluates to 180.

```
$x = 100 - 10 * 2;
$y = 100 - (10 * 2);
$z = (100 - 10) * 2;
```

Use Parentheses to Clarify Operator Precedence

Using parentheses to specify and clarify operator precedence is generally a good idea. It clarifies your intentions, makes your scripts easier to understand, and reduces errors.

As another example of using mathematical expressions, consider the following HTML document with a PHP script that calculates the average of three numbers. Figure 2.4 shows its output.

```
1.  <html>
2.  <head> <title>Expression Example </title> </head>
3.  <body>
4.  <?php
5.    $grade1 = 50;
6.    $grade2 = 100;
7.    $grade3 = 75;
8.    $average = ($grade1 + $grade2 + $grade3) / 3;
9.    print ("The average is $average");
10. ?> </body> </html>
```

Figure 2.4 Output of a Script That Calculates an Average

The following explanation covers the key lines from the script.

☆ Lines 5–7 set the initial values of the variables $grade1, $grade2, and $grade3.

☆ Line 8 calculates the average of the three variables, and then line 9 outputs the result.

◎◎ Working with PHP String Variables

So far, we have discussed variables with numeric values. As previously mentioned, variables can also be assigned character string values. Character strings are used in scripts to hold data such as customer names, addresses, product names, and descriptions. Consider the following example.

```
$name="Christopher";
$preference="Milk Shake";
```

Be careful when using expressions not to mix string and numeric variable types. For example, you might expect the following statements to generate an error message, but they will not. Instead, they will output "y=1".

```php
<?php
  $x ="banana";
  $sum = 1 + $x;
  print ("y=$sum");
?>
```

Here the variable $name is assigned the character string "Christopher" and the variable $preference is assigned "Milk Shake".

Unlike numeric variables, you cannot add, subtract, divide, or multiply string variables. PHP uses other methods to manipulate string variables. Two ways to manipulate strings are with string operators and with string functions. Let's examine the concatenate operator and then look at some common string functions.

Using the Concatenate Operator

Use the concatenate operator when you want to combine two separate string variables into one. The concatenate operator is specified as follows.

```php
$fullname = $firstname . $lastname;
```

Here the variable $fullname will receive the string values of $firstname and $lastname connected together. For example, consider the following partial PHP script.

```php
$firstname = "John";
$lastname = "Smith";
$fullname = $firstname . $lastname;
print ("Fullname=$fullname");
```

This script segment would output "Fullname=JohnSmith".

Using PHP String Functions

There are several different PHP applications that may require the use of string manipulation functions. Functions work much like operators, and you can use PHP string functions to do things like determine the length of strings, get subsets of strings, and remove leading space characters. One use of string manipulation functions might be to validate or alter input received from HTML forms. (Receiving data from HTML forms is described later in this chapter.) For example, you may need to determine the number of characters entered into an HTML form field or remove extra spaces entered.

The strlen() Function

Most string functions require you to send them one or more arguments. Arguments are input values that functions use in the processing they do. Often functions return a value to the script based on the input arguments. For example, consider the strlen() function (Figure 2.5), which accepts an argument as a string variable and returns the number of characters in the string.

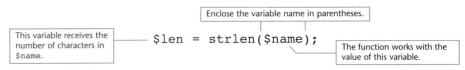

Figure 2.5 General Syntax of the `strlen()` Function

As an example of using the `strlen()` function, consider the following PHP script.

```php
<?php
    $comments = "Good Job";
    $len = strlen($comments);
    print ("Length=$len");
?>
```

This PHP script would output "Length=8".

The following subsections discuss the `trim()`, `strtolower()`, `strtoupper()`, and `substr()` PHP string functions and give examples of their usage.

The `trim()` Function

This function removes any blank characters from the beginning and end of a string. For example, consider the following script.

```php
<?php
    $in_name = "         Joe     Jackson          ";
    $name = trim($in_name);
    print ("name=$name$name");
?>
```

This PHP script would output "name=Joe   JacksonJoe   Jackson".

The `strtolower()` and `strtoupper()` Functions

These functions return the input string in all uppercase or all lowercase letters, respectively. For example, consider the following script.

```php
<?php
    $inquote = "Now Is The Time";
    $lower = strtolower($inquote);
    $upper = strtoupper($inquote);
    print ("upper=$upper lower=$lower");
?>
```

The above PHP script would output "upper=NOW IS THE TIME lower=now is the time".

The `substr()` Function

This function enables a PHP script to extract a portion of the characters in a string variable. It has the general syntax shown in Figure 2.6.

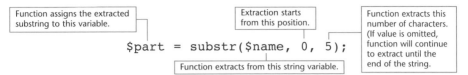

Figure 2.6 General Syntax of the `substr()` Function

The `substr()` function returns a substring from the string specified in the first argument. The function starts at a specific character position (the second argument) and extracts a specific number of characters (the third argument). If the third argument is omitted, then the `substr()` function will extract from the starting position (the second argument) until the end of the string.

It is important to note that the `substr()` function enumerates character positions starting with 0 (not 1), so, for example, in the string "Homer", the "H" would be position 0, the "o" would be position 1, the "m" position 2, and so on.

As an example, consider the following PHP script.

```php
<?php
    $date = "12/25/2002";
    $month = substr($date, 0, 2);
    $day = substr($date, 3, 2);
    print ("Month=$month Day=$day");
?>
```

The above PHP segment would output "Month=12 Day=25".

As another example, consider the following use of the `substr()` function that does not include the third argument (and thus returns a substring from the starting position to the end of the search string).

```php
<?php
    $date = "12/25/2002";
    $year = substr($date, 6);
    print ("Year=$year");
?>
```

The above script segment would output "Year=2002".

☆**TIP**   **Using a Negative Starting Value as a `substr()` Argument**

If you use a negative value for the second argument in the `substr()` function, the function will determine the starting position counting from the right end of the string instead of the left. For example, the following use of `substr()` extracts a substring that starts four characters from the end of the string.

```php
<?php
    $filename = "mydoc.html";
    $suffix = substr($filename, -4);
    print ("suffix=$suffix");
?>
```

The above script would output "suffix=html".

◎◎ Creating HTML Input Forms

So far the PHP scripts we have developed have been limited in that they cannot receive any input data from the user. That is, before we used any variable we had to explicitly set an initial value inside the script. HTML forms provide elements such as text areas, check boxes, selection lists, and radio buttons to provide input data for your PHP scripts. (See an example of an HTML form in Figure 2.7.) Although HTML forms are not a part of the PHP language, their use is important for creating input for PHP scripts. Let's review the various HTML form elements and then see how to use them to receive data into PHP scripts.

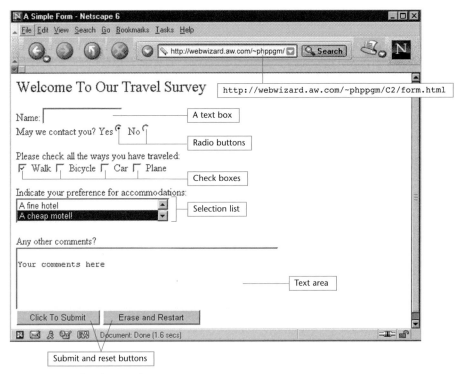

Figure 2.7 Example of a Simple HTML Form

Starting and Ending HTML Forms

You can create HTML forms by using the HTML `<form>` and `</form>` tags. Within these tags you place the various HTML form elements such as text areas, check boxes, and radio buttons. Figure 2.8 shows an example using the HTML `<form>` and `</form>` tags.

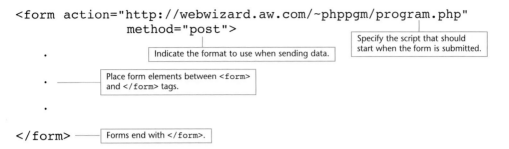

Figure 2.8 Format for Using the HTML `<form>` and `</form>` Tags

> The `<form>` tag has two primary arguments:
>
> 1. `action`. This option specifies the web address or URL of the script to start when the form is submitted. When the example form from Figure 2.8 is submitted, a script at Web address `http://webwizard.aw.com/~phppgm/program.php` will be started and it will be able to receive any input sent from the form.
>
> 2. `method`. This argument is set to either `post` or `get`. It defines the argument format to use to send data to the PHP script. The `get` method appends the form arguments to the end of the Web address. The `post` method sends the data as part of the body of the HTML document. Since the `get` method can limit the amount of data you can send, we will use the `post` method exclusively.

Creating Form Buttons

> Perhaps the most basic HTML form elements are form buttons, which enable the user to submit the form or erase all input and start again. When the user submits the form, it is sent to the location specified in the `action` argument of the `<form>` tag. HTML form buttons have the following format:

```
<input type="submit" value="Click To Submit">
<input type="reset" value="Erase and Restart">
```

Type of button to create   Button label

Figure 2.9 Format for Creating HTML Form Submit and Reset Buttons

> The HTML code in Figure 2.9 creates a submit button and a reset button. The submit button is labeled "Click To Submit" and the reset button is labeled "Erase and Restart."

☆**TIP**   **Another Argument for the Submit Button Form Element**

The submit button also has a `name` argument that is most commonly used when you have multiple submit buttons on a form and want to determine in the receiving script which button the user clicked.

To see a more complete example, consider the following script and its output in Figure 2.10. This script creates two buttons: a submit button and a reset button. When the form is submitted, it runs our initial PHP script from Chapter One, Figure 1.3 (saved at Web address `http://webwizard.aw.com/~phppgm/` `/First.php`). The top portion of Figure 2.10 shows the output form from the HTML code. The bottom of Figure 2.10 shows the output from `http://` `webwizard.aw.com/~phppgm/First.php` when the form is submitted.

```
1. <html>
2. <head> <title> A Simple Form </title> </head>
3. <body>
4. <form action="http://webwizard.aw.com/~phppgm/First.php"
       method="post" >
5.    Click submit to start our initial PHP program.
6.    <br> <input type="submit" value="Click To Submit">
7.    <input type="reset" value="Erase and Restart">
8. </form>
9. </body> </html>
```

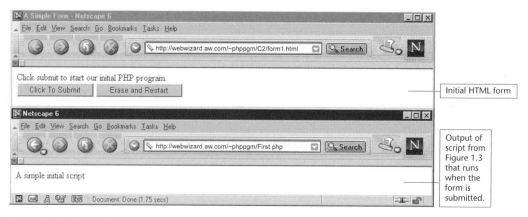

Figure 2.10 The Calling HTML Form (top) and the Output When the Form Is Submitted (bottom)

Let's briefly examine the key lines from this HTML document.

☆ Lines 1–3 create the HTML tags needed to start an HTML document.

☆ Line 4 starts the `<form>` tag and sets the `action` argument to start the script at `http://webwizard.aw.com/~phppgm/First.php`.

☆ Lines 6–7 create the submit and reset buttons.

☆ Lines 8–9 end the HTML form and HTML document.

Creating Text Input Boxes

Text input boxes create a form element for receiving a single line of text input. You can specify this form element within `<form>` and `</form>` tags as shown in Figure 2.11.

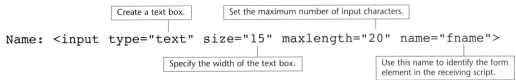

Figure 2.11 Format for Creating a Text Box HTML Form Element

The above HTML creates a text box 15 characters wide that will accept a maximum of 20 characters. It will set a variable named `fname` with value of whatever the end-user enters in the text box.

Creating Password Boxes

HTML supports creating text boxes as password areas instead of regular text boxes. Letters entered within a password box are viewed as asterisks (*) instead of the text being typed. To create a password box, set `type="password"` with the `input` form element tag. The other arguments of password boxes work much like those for text boxes. Figure 2.12 shows the HTML syntax used to create a password box within an HTML form. This example creates a password box that is 15 characters long and sets a variable called `pass1`.

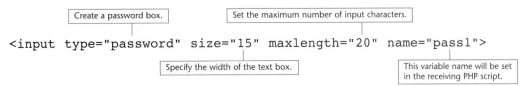

Figure 2.12 Format for Creating a Password Box HTML Form Element

> ☆**WARNING** **Password Boxes Are Not Secure**
>
> The HTML password box is not a secure method for transmitting passwords. When the user submits the form, any data input is sent in clear text (nonencrypted) just like any other HTML form field. Someone with network access could, therefore, read the password being transferred. For this reason, most Web applications do not use this approach to receive and transmit passwords.

Creating Text Areas

Text areas are similar to text boxes except that with text areas you can create multiple column and multiple row text-input areas. The HTML code shown in Figure 2.13 creates a text area containing 4 rows and 50 columns. The words "Your comments here" are the default text and will appear automatically in the text area when the form starts. The variable name `Comments` will be available to the form-handling script. Its value will be set to whatever the user enters into the text area.

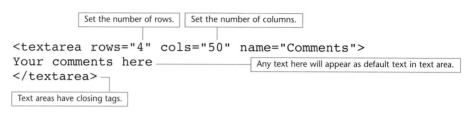

Figure 2.13 Format for Creating a Text Area HTML Form Element

Creating Radio Buttons

Radio buttons are small circles that the user can select by clicking them with a mouse. Only one button within a group can be selected at any given time. As with other form elements, the `name` argument creates a name for the element. The `name` argument must be the same for all radio buttons that you want to operate together as a group. The `value` argument sets the variable value that will be available to the form-processing script. Figure 2.14 shows how to create radio buttons with HTML.

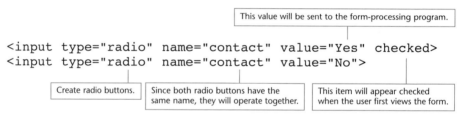

Figure 2.14 Format for Creating a Radio Button HTML Form Element

Creating Check Boxes

Check boxes are small boxes on a form that create a check mark when the user clicks them. The HTML lines shown in Figure 2.15 create four independent check boxes; that is, all four check box elements can be selected and each will set a value for a different variable name. For example, when the user clicks on the check box created in the second line, the variable `Bicycle` will have the value `Yes` in the receiving form-processing script.

```
This item will appear checked when the user first views the form.

<input type="checkbox" name="walk" value="Yes" checked> Walk
<input type="checkbox" name="Bicycle" value="Yes"> Bicycle
<input type="checkbox" name="Car" value="Yes"> Car
<input type="checkbox" name="Plane" value="Yes"> Plane
```

Create check boxes. Each check box sets a different variable name when selected. This value will be sent to the form-processing program.

Figure 2.15 Format for Creating a Check Box HTML Form Element

Sometimes you might want to create a set of check boxes that use the same `name` argument. Unlike radio buttons, when the same `name` argument is used within a group of check boxes, multiple check box elements can still be selected. The value received by the form-processing script would be a comma-separated list of all items checked. For example, if the *second* and *third* items in the check boxes shown in Figure 2.16 were checked, the form-processing script would receive a variable called `travel` with two comma-separated values: `"Bike,   Horse"`. (Receiving comma-separated values from a check box name variable is covered in Chapter Five.)

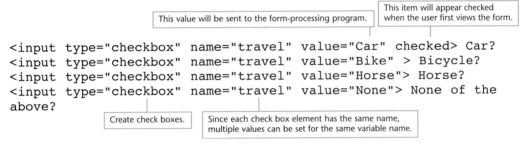

Figure 2.16 Format for Using Check Boxes with the Same `name` Argument

Creating Selection Lists

A selection list creates a box with a scrolling list of one or more items that the user can highlight and select. The entire list is enclosed in `<select>` and `</select>` tags. The `size` option defines how many lines will be displayed without scrolling. The `multiple` option allows more than one list item to be selected simultaneously. Within the `<select>` and `</select>` tags the HTML `<option>` tag defines each list option that will be displayed. The actual text displayed in the `<option>` tag is returned to the form-processing script through the variable specified in the `name` argument.

The HTML code shown in Figure 2.17 creates a selection list.

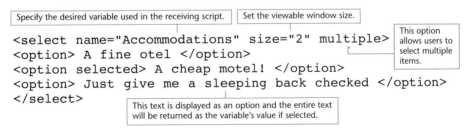

Figure 2.17 Format for Creating a Selection List HTML Form Element

This HTML code creates four options formatted in a scrolling list. Only two of these options are displayed at the same time, and the user can select more than one option. Multiple selections are sent to the form-processing script as a comma-separated list. (Receiving comma-separated lists in a PHP script is covered in Chapter Five.)

◎◎ Receiving Form Input into PHP Scripts

PHP makes it easy to receive input values from HTML forms. To receive input from HTML forms into your PHP script, use a PHP variable name that matches the variable defined in the form element's **name** argument. For example, assume the calling form uses a radio button with **name="contact"** as shown below.

```
<input type="radio" name="contact" value="Yes">
```

Then a form-handling PHP script can access the radio button's value by using a variable called **$contact**. In this case, if the user clicks the radio button, then when the form is submitted, **$contact** would have the value **Yes** in the receiving PHP script.

Consider the following full example of a PHP script receiving input from an HTML form that uses the following HTML form elements that create the variables **email** and **contact**.

```
Enter email address: <input type="text" size="16"
                            maxlength="20" name="email">
May we contact you?
<input type="radio" name="contact" value="Yes" checked> Yes
<input type="radio" name="contact" value="No"> No
```

The following script is placed into a file and stored at Web address http://webwizard.aw.com/~phppgm/C2/PrRadio.php (which matches the **action** argument of the calling form's **<form>** tag, not shown). The script will run when the form shown at the top of Figure 2.18 is submitted; the generated output appears at the bottom of Figure 2.18.

```
1. <html>
2. <head><title> Receiving Input </title> </head>
3. <body>
4. <font size="5">Thank You: Got Your Input.</font>
5. <?php
6.     print ("<br>Your email address is $email");
7.     print ("<br> Contact preference is $contact");
8. ?>
9. </body> </html>
```

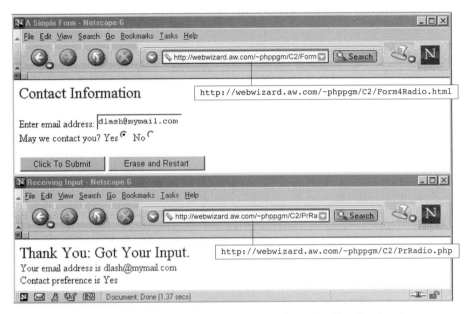

Figure 2.18 The HTML Input Form (top) and Output of a Script That Receives Input (bottom)

Here's a brief description of the script's key lines.

☆ Line 6 outputs the value of `$email` set from the calling form in the text box form element.

☆ Line 7 outputs the value of `$contact` set from the calling form in the radio button form element.

☆ **SHORTCUT** **Testing Input Values without HTML Forms**

You can send test input data to PHP scripts without a front-end HTML form by specifying data values in the URL box of a browser. For example, a test value for the variable `$email` for the script output in Figure 2.18 can be sent by appending `?email=dlash@dlash.com` to the Web address in the browser as follows:

`http://webwizard.aw.com/~phppgm/C2/PrRadio.php?email=dlash@dlash.com`

You can also send a test value for `$email` and `$contact` by appending `?email=dlash@dlash.com&Contact=No` to the Web address in the browser as follows:

`http://webwizard.aw.com/~phppgm/C2/PrRadio.php?email=dlash@dlash.com&contact=No`

Sending input values directly from a URL (without a front-end form) can provide a powerful way to test your scripts. It also means that any user might send variable values to your scripts without using your front-end forms. This capability of sending data from a URL means your scripts have to check Web input data carefully.

☆ Summary

▷ Variables are used to store and access data in computer memory. You can associate a value with a variable, change that value, print it out, and perform many different operations on it.

▷ PHP supports both numeric and string variables. String variables use different methods for value manipulation (for example, concatenation) than numeric variables do.

▷ You can use HTML forms to pass data to PHP scripts. Possible HTML form elements include text boxes, text areas, password boxes, check boxes, radio buttons, and selection lists, which allow users to input data for use in PHP scripts.

▷ PHP scripts can receive form element input values by using a PHP variable name that matches the one specified in the form element's `name` argument.

☆ Online References

HTML tutorial that includes a form overview
`http://www.htmlgoodies.com/`

PHP tutorial and overview information
`http://hotwired.lycos.com/webmonkey/`

Article discussing how to use PHP to read form variables
`http://www.devshed.com/Server_Side/PHP/Introduction/page3.html`

Tutorial discussing strings in PHP
`http://www.zend.com/zend/tut/using-strings.php`

☆ Review Questions

1. Which of the following are not valid PHP variable names?

   `$1st_counter, $x1, $soccer, $TimeCounter, squared`

   Why are they invalid?

2. What are the operator precedence rules in PHP? What would be the values of `$x` and `$y` after executing the following statements?

```php
<?php
    $x = 15 + 12 / 2 - 1;
    $y = (12 + 12) / 2 + 2;
?>
```

3. Name three numeric operators and three string manipulation functions.

4. What is the output of the following PHP code segment?

```php
<?php
    $x = 12; $y = 4;
    $num = $x + 8 / $y;
    print ("Num is $num but x is $x");
?>
```

5. What is the output of the following PHP code segment?

```php
<?php
    $x = 12; $y = 4; $z = 2;
    $num = $x * $z / $y;
    $x = $num * 2;
    print ("Num is $num but x is $x");
?>
```

6. What do the `trim()` and the `strtoupper()` functions do? What arguments do they use?

7. What is the output of the following PHP script?

```php
<?php
    $file = "    data.txt";
    $short = trim($file);
    $part = substr($short, 0, 4);
    $part2 = substr($short, -3);
    print ("part=$part part2=$part2");
?>
```

8. What is the difference between the text box, text area, and password box HTML form elements?

9. Suppose you must write a PHP script to receive input using the following HTML form element. What PHP variable name would you use, and what would be its value if it were checked?

```
<input type="checkbox" name="travel" value="Bike">
```

10. Suppose you must write a PHP script to receive input using the following HTML form element. What PHP variable name would you use? What would be the variable value if the user selected the third option?

```
<select name="Favorites" size="2" multiple>
<option> Baseball </option>
<option selected> Wild Parties </option>
<option> Camping in the Wilderness </option>
<option> Mountain Biking </option>
</select>
```

☆ Hands-On Exercises

1. Write scripts that calculate the following equations. Print out your results as HTML documents.

    a. Calculate the volume of a cylinder using the following formula

    $$V = \pi r^2 h$$

    Use $r = 4$ and $h = 12$. Use 3.14 as the value of π.

    b. Calculate the average of four grades, where `grade1` = 100, `grade2` = 75, `grade3` = 98, and `grade4` = 90.

2. Modify the script used in the example for Figure 2.3 to enable it to accept input from an HTML form. Create a front-end form that enables the user to set input values for ticket cost and building cost. After the script receives these values, output the total seats, total revenue, and total profit as shown in Figure 2.3.

3. Create a Web application that uses an HTML form to input the values of r and h used in Exercise 1a. Receive these values into a PHP script and output the results of the formula.

4. Create a form that includes a text box labeled `student_name` and four text boxes labeled `grade1`, `grade2`, `grade3`, and `grade4`. When the user enters his or her name and four grades, use a PHP script to return a new Web page with the user's name and average grade.

5. Create an HTML form that asks the user to enter a filename (from a text box on a form). Instruct the user to include a three-letter file suffix (for example, `.php`, `.txt`, or `.htm`). Create a receiving PHP script that outputs the file suffix (the last three characters of the filename) and the filename (all characters before the last four characters) that the user input. Remove any leading spaces that might be included.

6. Create a Web form that has the following form elements:
    - ✤ A text box for receiving a first name
    - ✤ Two radio buttons asking if the user purchases Internet access from an ISP (yes or no)
    - ✤ A checklist (with the same variable name set for each item) that asks the user to check all the different ways he or she has used the Web:
        - ✤ For research
        - ✤ To purchase items electronically
        - ✤ To send and receive e-mail
        - ✤ To read news

    Receive the above input into a PHP script and output all of the user's input. Also output the number of characters in his or her first name.

CHAPTER THREE

CONTROLLING SCRIPT FLOW

I f PHP scripts could only input data values, store them in variables, and operate on them, it would not be possible to solve many programming problems. For instance, a script could not determine whether one data value is larger than another nor sort a set of input values. To solve such programming problems, scripts need ways to test variable values and to repeat certain script lines. In this chapter we examine conditional test statements and looping statements that expand the types of problems we can solve.

◎◎ Chapter Objectives

⭐ To learn to use conditional test statements to compare numerical and string data values

⭐ To learn to use looping statements to repeat statements

⭐ To learn to use logical test operators to create compound conditional test statements

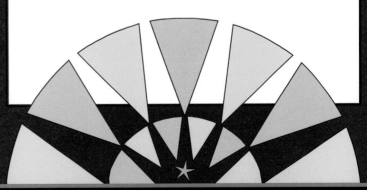

◎◎ Using Conditional Test Statements

Now that you've learned about using variables and receiving input values, let's look at a group of statements known as **conditional statements**. Conditional statements provide a way for scripts to test for certain data values and then to react differently depending on the value found. We will examine the `if` statement, the `elseif` clause, and the `else` clause, as well as the `switch` statement.

Using the if Statement

Use an `if` statement to specify a test condition and a set of statements to run when a test condition is *true*. Figure 3.1 shows its general format.

```
if ($average > 69) {
    $Grade="Pass";
    print "Grade=$Grade ";
}
print "Your average was $average";
```

> Execute these statements when the value of `$average` is greater than 69.

> Statements(s) to execute regardless of whether the test expression evaluates to *true* or *false*.

Figure 3.1 General Format of an `if` Statement

A **test expression** is enclosed in parentheses within an `if` statement. When the test expression evaluates to *true*, then one or more additional statements within the required curly brackets (`{ . . . }`) are carried out. When the test expression evaluates to *false*, then the script skips these statements. Regardless of whether the expression is *true* or *false*, any statements after the curly brackets are carried out.

Testing Numerical Values

Test expressions use **test operators** within their expressions. Test operators work much like the expression operators we studied in Chapter Two except test operators evaluate to *true* or *false*. For example, the `if` statement in Figure 3.1 uses the greater than (`>`) operator to test whether `$average` is greater than 69. Only when the value of `$average` is greater than 69 will the statements within the curly brackets be carried out.

Table 3.1 lists the common PHP test operators and gives an example of their use.

☆ **WARNING   Use == Not = in Test Conditions**

When testing whether one value is equal to another, be sure to use == (two equal signs) and not = (one equal sign). A single equal sign is an assignment operator and is always *true*. PHP will not give you a syntax error but the result will probably not be what you intended.

Table 3.1 Selected PHP Test Operators

Test Operator	Effect	Example	Result
==	Equal to	```if ($x == 6){\n $x = $y + 1;\n $y = $x + 1;\n}```	Run the second and third statements if the value of $x *is equal to* 6.
!=	Not equal to	```if ($x != $y) {\n $x = 5 + 1;\n}```	Run the second statement if the value of $x *is not equal to* the value of $y.
<	Less than	```if ($x < 100) {\n $y = 5;\n}```	Run the second statement if the value of $x *is less than* 100.
>	Greater than	```if ($x > 51) {\n print "OK";\n}```	Run the second statement if the value of $x *is greater than* 51.
>=	Greater than or equal to	```if (16 >= $x) {\n print "x=$x";\n}```	Run the second statement if 16 *is greater than or equal to* the value of $x.
<=	Less than or equal to	```if ($x <= $y) {\n print "y=$y";\n print "x=$x";\n}```	Run the second and third statements if the value of $x *is less than or equal to* the value of $y.

As an example of using test operators, consider the following script, which receives two grades as input and determines whether their average is above 89. It uses an HTML form for input (shown in the top of Figure 3.2). This HTML form uses the following form elements to request the user to enter input grades:

```
Enter First Score <input type="text" size="4"
                          maxlength="7" name="grade1">
Enter Second Score <input type="text" size="4"
                          maxlength="7" name="grade2">
```

When the user submits the form shown at the top of Figure 3.2, the following PHP script runs. Note that it outputs a message if the average of $grade1 and $grade2 is greater than 89. Regardless of the outcome of this conditional test, the script outputs the larger of $grade1 and $grade2.

```
1.  <html>
2.  <head><title>Decisions</title></head>
3.  <body>
4.  <?php
5.      $average = ($grade1 + $grade2) / 2;
6.      if ($average > 89){
7.          print "Average score: $average You got an A! <br>";
8.      }
9.      $max=$grade1;
10.     if ($grade1 < $grade2){
11.         $max = $grade2;
12.     }
13.     print ("Your max score was $max");
14. ?>
15. </body></html>
```

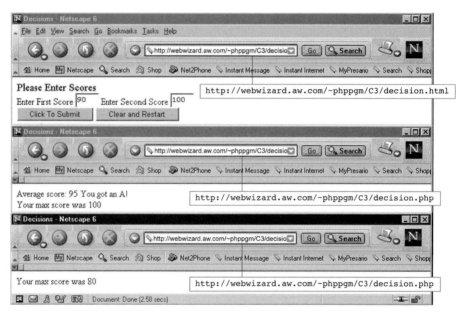

Figure 3.2 The Calling Form (top) and the Output When the Average of the Input Is Greater Than 89 (middle) and Less Than 90 (bottom)

Here's a summary of the key lines of this script.

☆ Line 5 calculates the average of `$grade1` and `$grade2`. Note that these values are passed from the calling form shown at the top of Figure 3.2.

☆ Lines 6–8 determine whether the average of `$grade1` and `$grade2` is greater than 89. If so, the script outputs a message indicating that the grade is an A.

Lines 9–13 check whether `$grade1` is less than `$grade2` and then outputs the larger value.

Comparing Strings

PHP represents string variable values using the **ASCII** (pronounced "ask-ee") code values. ASCII stands for American Standard Code for Information Interchange. It provides a standard, numerical way to represent characters on a computer. With the ASCII standard, every letter, number, and symbol is translated into a code number. For example, the character "A" is ASCII code 65, "B" is 66, "C" is 67, and so on. Also, the lowercase character "a" is ASCII code 97, "b" is 98, "c" is 99, and so on. Therefore, ASCII "A" is less than ASCII "a," "B" is less than "b," and "c" is less than "d." Finally, numbers represented as ASCII characters have ASCII code values lower than do letters. So, for example the ASCII character "1" is less than "a" or "A."

You can use == operator to check if one string is equal to another. For example, the following PHP segment compares if `$name1` is equal to `$name2`. It would output "George is not equal to Martha".

```
$name1 = "George";    $name2 = "Martha";
if ($name1 == $name2) {
   print ("$name1 is  equal to $name2");
} else {
   print ("$name1 is not equal to $name2");
}
```

You can also use the <, >, <=, and >= operators to compare string values using their ASCII code values. The results are what you would expect when comparing words alphabetically. For example the following PHP segment compares if `"George"` is less than `"Martha"`. It would output "George is less than Martha".

```
$name1 = "George";    $name2 = "Martha";
if ($name1 < $name2) {
   print ("$name1 is less than $name2");
} else {
   print ("$name1 is not less than $name2");
}
```

The following example compares two input strings. It uses the HTML form shown at the top of Figure 3.3, which has the following form element definition and sets the variables `first` and `second`.

```
First Name: <input type="text" size="10"
                    maxlength="15" name="first">
Second Name: <input type="text" size="10"
                    maxlength="15" name="second">
```

The following PHP script is called when the user submits the HTML form at the top of Figure 3.3. Sample outputs appear in the middle of Figure 3.3 (when "Football" and "Baseball" are entered) and at the bottom (when "Football" and "Soccer" are entered).

```
1.   <html>
2.   <head><title>String Comparison Results</title></head>
3.   <body>
4.   <?php
5.   print ("First=$first Second=$second<br>");
6.   if ($first == $second) {
7.       print ("$first and $second are equal");
8.   }
9.   if ($first < $second) {
10.      print ("$first is less than $second");
11.  }
12.  if ($first > $second) {
13.      print ("$first is greater than $second");
14.  }
15.  ?></body></html>
```

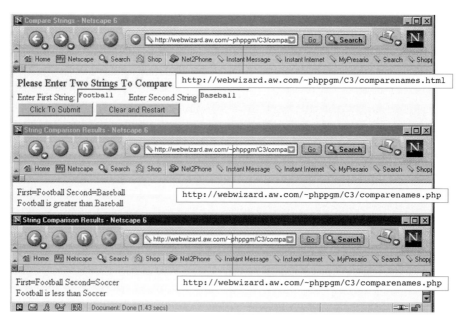

Figure 3.3 The Calling Form (top) and the Output When the User Enters "Football" and "Baseball" (middle) and "Football" and "Soccer" (bottom)

The following describes the key lines from the above script:

☆ Line 6 checks if variables `$first` and `$second` have the same value.

☆ Lines 9–11 check if `$first` has an ASCII code value less than `$second`.

☆ Lines 12–14 check if `$first` has an ASCII code value higher than `$second`.

☆**TIP**   Using `strcmp()` and `strcasecmp()` functions

You can also use the `strcmp()` and `strcasecmp()` functions to perform case-sensitive and case-insensitive string variable comparisons. These functions use two arguments that are the two strings to compare. Based on the comparison they return:

✦ A positive value if the *first* string is greater than the *second*
✦ A negative value if the *first* string is less than the *second*
✦ Zero if the two string values are equal

Therefore, the script line below performs a case-insensitive comparison and would return 0 into the variable $num.

```
$num = strcasecmp("Spring Break", "spring break");
```

You can omit the test expression when you are checking whether the output of a function is not zero. For example, the following script concisely performs a case-sensitive check whether the string `$first` is not equal to `$second`.

```
if (strcmp($first, $second)) {
    print "$first is not equal to $second";
}
```

Using the elseif Clause

Use an `elseif` clause with an `if` statement to specify an additional test condition to check when the previous test conditions are *false*. This clause also gives one or more statements to run when its test condition is *true*. The PHP `elseif` clause has the general format shown in the `if-elseif` statement in Figure 3.4.

```
if (test expression) {
    one or more PHP statements
} elseif (test expression) {
    one or more PHP statements
}
```

When run, the script checks the `elseif` test expression when the test condition for the `if` statement is *false*.

Statements between curly brackets run when the `elseif` test expression is *true*.

Enclose the PHP statements in curly brackets.

Figure 3.4 General Format of an `if-elseif` Statement

One or more elseif clauses can be used with a single `if` statement. For example, consider the following PHP code segment that uses multiple `elseif` clauses.

```php
if ($hour < 9) {
    print "Sorry, it is too early.";
} elseif ($hour < 12) {
    print "Good morning. The hour is $hour. ";
    print "How can we help you?";
} elseif ($hour < 13) {
    print "Sorry, we are out to lunch. ";
} elseif ($hour < 17) {
    print "Good afternoon. The hour is $hour. ";
    print "How can we help you?";
} elseif ($hour <= 23) {
    print "Sorry, we have gone home already.";
}
```

Check this test expression when the first test expression is *false*.

Check this test expression when the first two test expressions are *false*.

Check this test expression when the first three conditions are all *false*.

Each `elseif` test expression is evaluated only when the previous test expressions are all *false*. For example, if `$hour` has a value of 15, this code outputs "Good afternoon. The hour is 15. How can we help you?" However, if `$hour` has a value of 24, then this code outputs nothing.

Using the else Clause

Use an `else` clause with an `if` statement and possibly one or more `elseif` clauses. It specifies an additional set of statements to run when all the previous test expressions are *false*. The PHP `else` clause has the general format shown in the `if-else` statement in Figure 3.5.

```php
if (test expression) {
    one or more PHP statements
} else {
    one or more PHP statements
}
```

Enclose the PHP statements in curly brackets.

This set of statements runs when the test expression for the `if` statement is *false*.

Figure 3.5 General Format of an `if-else` Statement

You can use an `else` clause with an `if` statement and one or more `elseif` clauses. For example, the next PHP code segment uses an `else` clause with an `if` statement and two `elseif` clauses.

```php
if ($count == 0) {
    print ("Time to reorder.");
    $reorder=1;
} elseif ($count == 1) {
    $reorder=1;
    print ("Warning: we need to start reordering.");
```

```
} elseif ($count > 1) {
    $reorder = 0;
    print ("We are OK for now.");
} else {
    print ("Illegal value for count = $count");
}
```

> This statement executes when all previous test conditions are *false*.

The `else` clause above is carried out only when all the previous test expressions are *false*. For example, if `$count` had a value of –75, then this code would output "Illegal value for count = –75" only after checking whether `$count` was equal to 0, whether `$count` was equal to 1, and then whether `$count` was greater than 1.

As a full example of using `elseif` and `else` clauses, let's extend the grade-averaging script from Figure 3.2 to determine a letter grade (A, B, C, D, or F) and to catch illegal input. The script uses the HTML form for input shown at the top of Figure 3.6 and uses the following form elements to set the variables `grade1` and `grade2`.

```
Enter First Score <input type="text" size="4"
                          maxlength="7" name="grade1">
Enter Second Score <input type="text" size="4"
                          maxlength="7" name="grade2">
```

When the user submits the form shown at the top of Figure 3.6, the following PHP script runs. The middle screen shows the output when the user inputs 70 for `$grade1` and 90 for `$grade2`. The bottom of Figure 3.6 shows the output when the user inputs 0 for `$grade1` and –1 for `$grade2`.

```
1.   <html>
2.   <head><title>Grade Calculation</title></head>
3.   <body>
4.   <?php
5.   $average = ($grade1 + $grade2) / 2;
6.   if ($average > 89) {
7.       print ("Average=$average You got an A");
8.   } elseif ($average > 79) {
9.       print ("Average=$average You got a B");
10.  } elseif ($average > 69) {
11.      print ("Average=$average You got a C");
12.  } elseif ($average > 59) {
13.      print ("Average=$average You got a D");
14.  } elseif ($average >= 0) {
15.      print ("Grade=$grade You got an F");
```

> Compute the average of $grade1 and $grade2.

> Check whether the grade average is an A, B, C, D, or F mark.

```
16. } else {
17.     print ("Illegal average less than 0 average=$average");
18. }
19. $max=$grade1;
20. if ($grade1 < $grade2) {
21.     $max = $grade2;
22. }
23. print ("<br>Your max score was $max");
24. ?> </body></html>
```

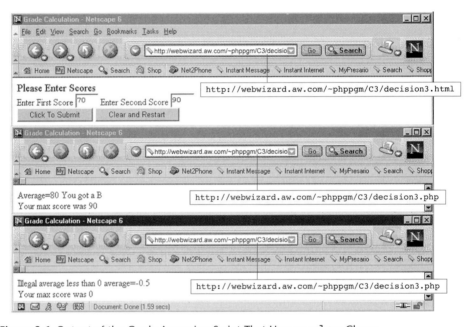

Figure 3.6 Output of the Grade-Averaging Script That Uses an `else` Clause

The following summary describes the key statements from the script.

☆ Line 5 calculates the average of `$grade1` and `$grade2`. Note that these values are passed from the calling form shown at the top of Figure 3.6.

☆ Lines 6–7 determine whether the average of `$grade1` and `$grade2` is greater than 89. If so, the script outputs a message indicating that the grade is an A.

☆ Lines 8–15 determine whether the average of `$grade1` and `$grade2` is between 0 and 89. If so, the script outputs a letter grade of B, C, D, or F, depending on the average.

☆ If all of the other `if-elseif` test conditions are *false*, lines 16–17 output a message that indicates the input is illegal.

Using the PHP Ternary Operator

PHP supports the **ternary operator** (sometimes called ?:) as a very concise way to do a conditional test with a single if and else statement. It has the following general format.

```
expression1 ? statement2 : statement3;
```

The above statement evaluates expression1: if *true*, the script runs statement2; if *false*, the script runs statement3. So, for example, the following code would output "x greater than 4".

```
<?php
$x = 5;
( $x > 4 ) ? print "x greater than 4" : print "x not more than 4";
?>
```

Using the switch Statement

In some cases, you can use the switch statement as a more convenient conditional test construct than multiple if-elseif-else statements. You can use it to select a set of statements to run depending on a variable's value. For example, the following switch statement carries out different code sections depending on the value of $rating.

```
switch ($rating) {        Enclose the switch statement in curly brackets.
    case 1:
        $rated = "Poor";
        print "The rating was $rated";        Run these statements when $rating has value 1.
        break;
    case 2:
        $rated = "Fair";
        print "The rating was $rated";        Run these statements when $rating has value 2.
        break;
    case 3:
        $rated = "Good";
        print "The rating was $rated";        Run these statements when $rating has value 3.
        break;
    default:
        print "Error: that rating does not exist";        Run this statement only when $rating does not have values 1, 2, or 3.
}
```

The above switch statement tests the value of $rating and, depending on its value, runs the statements in the appropriate case statement. If, for example, $rating has value 3, then the above code would output "The rating was Good". If $rating does not have a value of 1, 2 or 3, then the above code would output "Error: that rating does not exist". The break statement used in each case block is needed to send control out of the switch block to the next statement after the switch statement block.

Using Loops to Repeat Statements

PHP supports three program constructs that enable scripts to repeat sections of code. By repeating sections of code with loops, you can achieve these goals.

⭐ *Your scripts can be much more concise.* When similar sections of statements need to be repeated in your script, you can often put them into a loop and reduce the total number of lines of code required.

⭐ *You can write more flexible scripts.* Loops allow you to repeat sections of your script until you reach the end of a data structure such as a list (see Chapter Five) or a file (see Chapter Six). Without a looping structure, you would need to know the number of list elements or the length of the file in advance.

PHP supports three types of looping constructs:

1. The `for` loop

2. The `while` loop

3. The `foreach` loop

We describe the `for` and `while` loops below. We defer discussion of the `foreach` loop until the arrays section in Chapter Five.

Using the for Loop

Use the `for` loop to repeat a section of code a specified number of times. It has the general format shown in Figure 3.7.

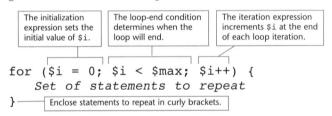

Figure 3.7 General Format of the `for` Loop

Figure 3.7 repeats the set of designated statements `$max` times. The number of repetitions of the loop is controlled by the three parts of the `for` statement.

1. *The initialization expression* defines the initial value of a variable used to control the loop. In Figure 3.7, the variable `$i` is used to control the loop; it has an initial value of 0.

2. *The loop-end condition* defines the condition that triggers the termination of the loop. The valid test conditions are the same as those shown in Table 3.1. The condition is evaluated at the beginning of each loop iteration. When it

evaluates to *false*, the loop ends. In Figure 3.8, the loop will repeat as long as $i is less than $max.

3. *The iteration expression* is evaluated at the end of each loop iteration. In Figure 3.7, the expression $i++ tells PHP to add 1 to the value of $i at the end of each loop iteration. Another common iteration expression is $i--, which subtracts 1 from the value of $i.

☆**WARNING** Semicolon Use in `for` Statements

Look carefully at the syntax of the `for` loop. A semicolon (;) is required after the initialization expression (first part) and the loop-end condition (second part) of the `for` statement, but a semicolon is not used after the iteration expression (the third part), as shown in Figure 3.7. Placing a semicolon after the iteration expression of the `for` loop in Figure 3.7 would result in a syntax error.

Inside the loop, the value of $i changes during each iteration. In Figure 3.7, this variable would have a value of 0 in the first iteration, 1 in the second iteration, 2 in the third iteration, and so on.

As an example, the following script demonstrates the use of a `for` loop while generating an HTML form. The form asks the user to select start and end numbers. When the user submits the form the input data is sent to http:// webwizard.aw.com/~phppgm/C3/whileloop.php. The script below uses a `for` loop to concisely generate a set of options for the HTML <select> form elements. Figure 3.8 shows the output form.

```
1.   <html><head><title>Loops</title></head>
2.   <body><font size="5" color="blue">
3.   Generate Square and Cube Values </font>
4.   <br>
5.   <form action="http://webwizard.aw.com/~phppgm/C3/
     whileloop.php" method="post">
6.   <?php
7.
8.       print ("Select Start Number");
9.       print ("<select name=\"start\">");
10.      for ($i=0; $i<10; $i++) {
11.          print ("<option>$i</option>");
12.      }
13.      print ("</select>");
14.      print ("<br>Select End Number");
15.      print ("<select name=\"end\">");
16.      for ($i=10; $i<20; $i++) {
17.          print "(<option>$i</option>)";
18.      }
19.      print ("</select>");
20.
21.  ?>
```

Repeat print statement 10 times with values 0, 1, 2, ... 9 for $i.

Repeat print statement 10 times with values 10, 11, 12, ... 19 for $i.

```
22. <br><input type="submit"  value="Submit">
23. <input type="reset"  value="Clear and Restart">
24. </form></body></html>
```

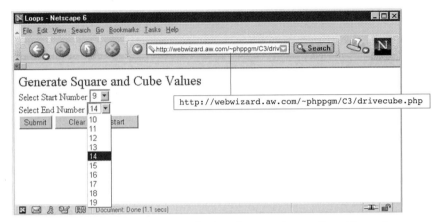

Figure 3.8 Using a `for` Loop to Generate Options for a `<select>` Form Element

The following summarizes some of the key lines from the script.

☆ Lines 1–5 start the HTML document and set the form's output to be sent to `http://webwizard.aw.com/~phppgm/C3/whileloop.php`.

☆ Lines 9–12 start the `<select>` HTML form element that sets optional values for `start`. A `for` loop creates 10 options with values from 0 to 9.

☆ Lines 15–18 start the `<select>` HTML form element that sets the optional values of `end`. A `for` loop creates 10 options with values from 10 to 19.

Using the while Loop

Use the `while` loop to repeat a section of code as long as a test condition remains *true*. It has the general format shown in Figure 3.9.

Enclose the test condition in parentheses.	The loop repeats as long as the conditional test is *true*.

```
while ($ctr < $max) {
    Set of statements to repeat
}
```

Figure 3.9 General Format of a `while` Loop

The loop shown in Figure 3.9 will continue looping as long as the loop conditional test is *true*. If the loop conditional test is initially *false*, then the statements within the loop body will never run.

☆**WARNING** Infinite Loops

If the conditional test of a while loop is always *true*, then the loop will never end. Creating such an **infinite loop** is generally a bad idea. It will consume resources on the Web server and possibly slow down other server activity. If you accidentally set up an infinite loop, you might have to exit the window that's running your script (that is, the MS-DOS window, Telnet window, or Web browser) to terminate your script.

Figure 3.10 shows a full example using a while loop that outputs a table of square and cube values. The script receives as input the variables start and end set from the calling form (shown in Figure 3.8). The sample output appears in Figure 3.10.

```
1.  <html>
2.  <head><title>While Loop</title></head>
3.  <body>
4.  <font size="4" color="blue"> Table of Square and Cube Values
    </font>
5.  <table border=1>
6.  <th> Numb </th> <th> Sqr </th> <th> Cubed </th>
7.  <?php
8.      $i = $start;
9.      while ($i <= $end) {
10.         $sqr=$i*$i;
11.         $cubed=$i*$i*$i;
12.         print ("<tr><td>$i</td><td>$sqr</td>
                <td>$cubed</td></tr>");
13.         $i = $i + 1;
14.     }
15. ?></table></body></html>
```

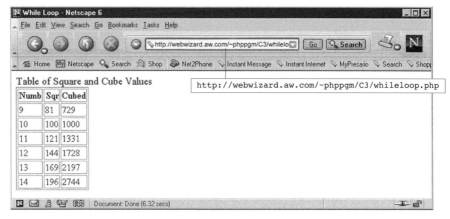

Figure 3.10 Using a while Loop to output a table of square and cube values

Here's a summary of some of the key lines of the script.

☆ Lines 5–6 start the HTML table and output the initial table headers.

☆ Line 8 sets the initial value for the variable `$i` to be the starting value input in the HTML form. Line 9 begins the `while` loop, setting it to iterate as long as the value of `$i` is less than or equal to the value of `$end`.

☆ Lines 10–14 form the body of the `while` loop. They calculate the square and cube values of `$i` and output them as part of a table row. Note that line 13 increments the value of `$i` for each iteration of the loop.

☆WARNING Checking Input Variables

The script that results in the output shown in Figure 3.10 is a good example of a script that should check input more carefully. When you write any script that accepts input from a user, you need to carefully consider how your script will handle illegal input even when you expect input to come from your own front-end form. For example, by using the command below, a user might send argument values via a URL instead of using the form.

```
http://webwizard.aw.com/~phppgm/C3/whileloop.php?start=zero&end=million
```

☆TIP   Using Either the `while` Loop or the `for` Loop for Some Problems

For some loops you can use either the `while` loop or the `for` loop. For example, the following two loops both output "i=0 i=1 i=2 i=3 i=4".

```
for ($i=0; $i<5; $i++) { print "i=$i "; }
$i = 0; while ($i < 5) { print  "i=$i "; $i=$i + 1; }
```

Later when we study arrays and files, we'll see situations where `while` loops work better than `for` loops.

☆ SHORTCUT Putting a Test Condition at the End of a Loop

Sometimes you may want to ensure your `while` loop runs at least once. PHP also supports placing a `while` test condition at the end of the loop, as shown below.

```
do {
    Statements to repeat
} while (test condition);
```

This loop works the same as the `while` loop we just examined, except the text condition is not evaluated and checked until the bottom of the loop.

◎◎ Using Logical Test Operators

PHP supports a set of logical test operators you can use to create compound test expressions. They are typically used within an `if` statement or a `while` statement to specify more than one test condition. For example, consider the following line of code, which will loop as long as `$x > $max` *and* `$found` is not equal to 1.

Using Logical Test Operators *(sidebar tab)*

```
while ($x > $max && $found != 1) {
```

PHP supports three logical test operators.

1. `&&`—*the AND operator.* This operator is used to create a compound test condition in `if` statements and `while` loops. It enables you to create a statement like the following:

```
while ($ctr < $max && $flag == 0) {
```

This statement repeats the statements in its loop as long as `$ctr` is less than `$max` and `$flag` is equal to 0. Whenever either of these expressions is *false,* the loop will terminate.

2. `||`—*the OR operator.* This operator is used much like the AND operator; that is, it is primarily used to create a compound test condition in `if` statements and `while` loops. It enables you to create statements like the following:

```
if ($ctr != $max  || $flag == 0) {
```

This statement carries out the statements within the `if` statement if either `$ctr` is not equal to `$max` or `$flag` is equal to 0.

3. `!`—*the NOT operator.* This operator is used to test whether an expression is *false.* It can be used in `while` loops and in `if` statements. Here is an example:

```
if (!$flag == 0) {
```

This statement is *true* when `$flag` has any value except 0.

☆ **SHORTCUT** **Checking If Input Variables Are Empty**

Often you may want to verify that the user entered a value in a form element from an input form (and did not submit the form to your script with the field blank). You can use the logical OR operator to concisely check whether input from form text fields have been supplied to your PHP script. For example, the following script segment checks whether `$last` and `$first` have empty values.

```
if (($last == '') || ($first == '')) {
    print "Error missing either first or last";
}
```

An alternative, even more concise style would use the NOT operator with the OR operator as shown below.

```
if ( !$last  || !$first ) {
    print "Error missing either first or last";
}
```

The following example, which asks the user to guess a "secret" two-digit combination, uses logical test operators. The input form shown at the top of Figure 3.11 calls the script. The HTML form uses the following group of radio buttons to set `pick1`. A similar group of radio buttons sets a second variable named `pick2`.

```
<font size="4"> Pick a number from 1 to 9 <br>
<input type="radio" name="pick1" value="1">1
<input type="radio" name="pick1" value="2">2
<input type="radio" name="pick1" value="3">3
<input type="radio" name="pick1" value="4">4
<input type="radio" name="pick1" value="5">5
<input type="radio" name="pick1" value="6">6
<input type="radio" name="pick1" value="7">7
<input type="radio" name="pick1" value="8">8
<input type="radio" name="pick1" value="9">9
```

In the receiving PHP script shown below, note the use of the compound logical tests in lines 6 and 8. The output when the user guesses one of the two numbers correctly is shown in the middle of Figure 3.11, and the bottom of the figure shows the output when the user guesses both numbers correctly.

```
1.   <html><head><title>Number Guess Results </title><head>
2.   <body>
3.   <?php
4.       $combo1=5;
5.       $combo2=6;
6.       if (($pick1 == $combo1) && ($pick2 == $combo2)) {
7.       print ("Congratulations you got both secret numbers
         $combo1 $combo2!");
8.       } elseif (($pick1 == $combo1) || ($pick2 == $combo2)){
9.       print ("You got one number right.");
10.      } else {
11.      print ("Sorry, you are totally wrong!");
12.      }
13.      print ("You guessed $pick1 and $pick2.");
14.  ?></body></html>
```

This statement is *true* if $pick1 equals $combo1 AND $pick2 equals $combo2.

This statement is *true* if EITHER $pick1 equals $combo1 OR $pick2 equals $combo2.

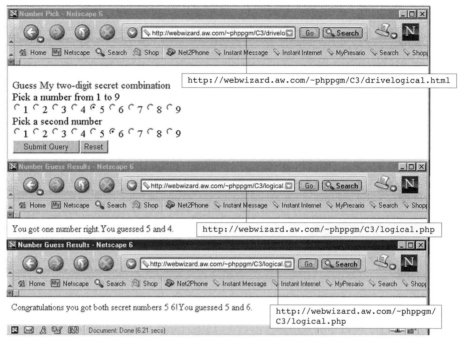

Figure 3.11 The Input Form (top) and the Output with One Number (middle) and Two Numbers (bottom) of the Secret Combination Guessed Correctly

Here's a brief description of the key lines of the script.

☆ Lines 4–5 set the secret numbers to be 5 and 6.

☆ Line 6 uses a logical AND operator to determine whether both $pick1 and $pick2 (set in the calling form) are correct.

☆ Line 8 uses a logical OR operator to determine whether either $pick1 or $pick2 are correct.

☆**WARNING Use Compound Conditionals Carefully**

Use caution when including compound conditionals in your scripts since they can be tricky and can introduce errors into a script's logic. When you use compound conditionals, it's a good idea to create test cases to test each targeted condition independently.

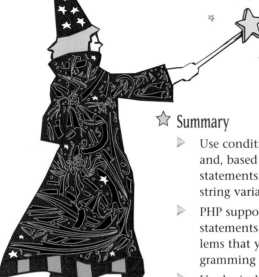

☆ Summary

▷ Use conditional statements to test for certain conditions and, based on the results of the test, to run specific script statements. PHP provides ways to test both numerical and string variables.

▷ PHP supports loops which allow scripts to repeat a set of statements. Loops expand the types of programming problems that you can solve and allow you to solve some programming problems more concisely.

▷ Use logical AND (&&), OR (||) and NOT (!) operators to carry out compound tests within a conditional test statement.

☆ Online References

PHP resource site with functions, partial scripts, and documentation
`http://php.resourceindex.com`

A PHP tutorial section discussing control structures
`http://www.gimpster.com/php/tutorial/control-structures.php`

PHP scripts and documentation
`http://www.1phpstreet.com`

☆ Review Questions

1. What three types of conditional clauses were described in this chapter? Which is the only one that can be used by itself?

2. Which test operator is used to test whether one of two numerical variables is greater than the other? Which test operator is used to test whether one of two numerical variables is equal to the other?

3. What operators should you use to compare string variables? What is `strcmp()` used for? What are the three possible output values from the `strcmp()` function?

4. What is the value of `$i` after running the following PHP code segment?

```
$i = 12; $j = 10;
if ($i < $j) {
    $i = $i + 1;
} elseif ($i > $j) {
    $i = $i + 2;
} else { $i = 6;
}
```

5. What are two advantages of using looping statements? Name two types of looping constructs discussed in this chapter.

6. What are the three parts of the `for` loop?

7. How many times will the following loop repeat?

```
for ( $i=6; $i<10; $i++ ) {
    $i=$i + 1;
}
```

8. What would be the output of the script associated with Figure 3.10 if the value of $i is greater than $end from the start of the script?

9. What would be the output of the following code?

```
$ctr=5; $ctr2=0;
while ($ctr < 10 || $ctr2 <= 7) {
    $ctr = $ctr + 1;
    $ctr2 = $ctr + 1;
    print "ctr=$ctr ctr2=$ctr2";
}
```

10. How many times will the following loop repeat?

```
$flag = 0; $ctr=0;
while (!$flag) {
    $ctr = $ctr + 1;
    if ($ctr > 3) {
        $flag = 1;
    }
}
```

☆ Hands-On Exercises

1. Modify the script whose output is shown in Figure 3.2 to include the following changes.

   a. Output the following message when the average of the two grades is 100: "Congratulations on your perfect score."

   b. Output the following additional message when the average of the two grades is less than 50: "Please see your instructor for help."

2. Modify the script whose output is shown in Figure 3.6 to include the following tests.

   a. Check whether either `$grade1` or `$grade2` is greater than 100. If so, output an error message and exit the script.

   b. Check whether either `$grade1` or `$grade2` is less than 0. If so, output an error message and exit the script.

   c. Check whether either `$grade1` or `$grade2` is less than 70. If so, output the following message: "Please see your instructor for help."

3. Write a script that accepts two arguments, `totdebt` and `income`, from an input HTML form.

   a. If the total debt is less than 15% of income, generate an HTML document in green font and font size 4 that says, "Credit is approved." Output the total debt, total income, and amount of debt as a percentage of total income.

   b. If total debt is between 15% and 30% of income, generate an HTML document in blue font and font size 4 that says, "Credit is borderline." Output the total debt, total income, and amount of debt as a percentage of total income.

   c. If total debt is more than 30% of income, generate an HTML document in red font and font size 4 that says, "Credit is NOT APPROVED." Output the total debt, total income, and amount of debt as a percentage of total income.

   Test your script with the following values. Make sure your script works appropriately for each set.

   i. `totdebt` = 25,000, `income` = 100,000
   ii. `totdebt` = 7,500, `income` = 15,000
   iii. `totdebt` = 0, `income` = 50,000
   iv. `totdebt` = 125,000, `income` = 50,000
   v. `totdebt` = 0, `income` = 0
   vi. `totdebt` = –50, `income` = –100

4. Create a multiple-choice Web-based exam that includes four questions with the following properties.

   ✩ Each question has at least four choices labeled A, B, C, and D. (Make up the questions yourself.)

   ✩ The correct answers should be: question 1: A, question 2: B, question 3: C, and question 4: D.

   ✩ When the user submits the form, score the questions and output the overall percentage of correct answers. In the output, indicate which answers were wrong.

5. Modify the script whose output appears in Figure 3.10 to also output the looping variable raised to the fourth and fifth powers. Also include a check to ensure that the value of `$start` is from 0 to 9 and the value of `$end` is from 10 to 19.

6. Modify the script whose output appears in Figure 3.11 to become a four-number combination instead of a two-number combination. Use 9, 6, 3, 1 as the set of combination numbers.

CHAPTER FOUR

POWERING YOUR SCRIPTS WITH FUNCTIONS

Beyond the string manipulation functions we discussed in Chapter Two, PHP supports several other functions useful for Web application development. This chapter describes how to use functions to perform tasks such as generating random numbers, obtaining dates and times, and testing whether an input variable is a valid number. We also discuss creating and using your own custom functions, covering how to create a function, pass it arguments, return values, alter argument values, and create and use functions in external files.

Chapter Objectives

⭐ To learn to use several PHP functions useful for Web application development

⭐ To learn to write and use your own functions

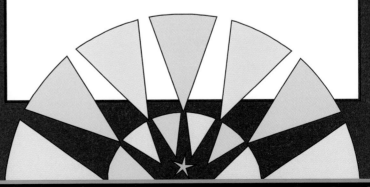

◎◎ More on Using Basic PHP Functions

In Chapter Two you learned how to use functions as a way to manipulate string variables. We discussed functions such as `strlen()`, `trim()`, `strtolower()`, `strtoupper()`, and `substr()`. In this section we examine several other functions useful for building PHP Web applications, including the following topics:

☆ Some basic numeric PHP functions—We will discuss the absolute value [`abs()`], square root [`sqrt()`], round [`round()`], integer checker [`is_numeric()`], and random number generation [`rand()`] functions.

☆ The `print()` function—We will cover more details about the capabilities of the `print()` function.

☆ The `date` function—We will discuss using the `date()` function to determine date and time information.

Some Basic PHP Functions

Let's look at some simple numeric PHP functions you may find useful when writing your own scripts.

The abs() Function

The absolute value function takes a single numerical argument and returns its absolute value. For example, the code below produces the output "x=5 y=42".

```
$x=abs(-5);
$y=abs(42);
print "x=$x y=$y";
```

The sqrt() Function

The square root function takes a single numerical argument and returns its square root. For example, the code below produces the output "x=5 y=4.898979485566".

```
$x=sqrt(25);
$y=sqrt(24);
print "x=$x y=$y";
```

The round() Function

The round function takes a single numerical argument and returns the number rounded up or down to the nearest integer. For example, the code below produces the output "x=-5 y=4".

```
$x=round(-5.456);
$y=round(3.7342);
print "x=$x y=$y";
```

You can also specify a second argument for the `round()` function that indicates the number of digits after the decimal point to round to. For example, the code below produces the output "x=-5.46 y=3.734".

```
$x=round(-5.456,2);
$y=round(3.7342,3);
print "x=$x y=$y";
```

The is_numeric() Function

The is_numeric() function is useful for determining whether a variable is a valid number or a numeric string. It returns *true* or *false*. Use this function to verify whether input from a calling form (for example, from a text box form element) is a valid number or not. Consider the following example.

```
if (is_numeric($input)) {
    print "Got Valid Number=$input";
} else {
    print "Not Valid Number=$input";
}
```

If $input had value "6" then the following would be output:

```
Got Valid Number=6
```

If $input had value "Happy" then the above script would output:

```
Not Valid Number=Happy
```

The rand() Function

Use the rand() function to generate a random number. Your script can use random numbers in many ways such as to simulate a dice roll or a coin toss or to randomly select an advertisement banner to display. You typically send the rand() function two arguments that define the range of numbers it should return (minimum and maximum limits, respectively). So the following call to rand() returns a random number from 1 to 15 inclusive.

```
$num = rand(1, 15);
```

Before your first call to rand() in a script, use the srand() function to "seed" the random number generator and help ensure rand() returns a truly random number. The PHP manual recommends that you use the following line to call srand(), which uses the output from the microtime() function multiplied by 10,000,000 to establish a unique input argument for srand().

```
srand ((double) microtime() * 10000000);
```

Here is an example of using rand() with the srand() function.

```
srand ((double) microtime() * 10000000);
$dice = rand(1, 6);
print "Your random dice toss is $dice";
```

The random number generated in this case can be a 1, 2, 3, 4, 5, or 6. Thus one possible output of this code is "Your random dice toss is 3".

☆**WARNING Call `srand()` Only Once Per Script**

The PHP manual strongly recommends that you use `srand()` once per script. Multiple calls to `srand()` can result in the return of nonrandom numbers. So if your script is generating multiple random numbers, call `srand()` once and then make multiple calls to `rand()`.

☆**TIP   Other PHP Numerical Functions**

PHP supports a full set of numerical functions, including tangent [`tan()`], cosine [`cosin()`], sine [`sin()`], round up [`ceiling()`], round down [`floor()`], and exponentiation [`pow()`]. See the online manual (`http://www.php.net/math`) for details on these functions.

The `print()` Function

Although we have already been using the `print()` function, we have not discussed its different output forms. For example, you can enclose your output statements in parentheses or omit the parentheses completely. (In most of this book, we do not use the parentheses in the `print()` function.) You can also use single or double quotation marks to enclose the output. You have already seen that when you use double quotation marks, PHP searches through the string and outputs the values of any variables. For example, the following PHP segment uses double quotation marks.

```
$x = 10;
print ("Mom, please send $x dollars");
```

Therefore it would output the following: "Mom, please send 10 dollars".

If you want to output the actual variable name (and not its value), use single quotation marks. For example, the following script fragment uses single quotation marks.

```
$x = 10;
print ('Mom, please send $x dollars');
```

It would output the following message: "Mom, please send $x dollars".

If you want to output the value of only a single variable or expression, you can omit the quotation marks.

```
$x=5;
print $x*3;
```

This statement would output "15".

☆ SHORTCUT **Generating HTML Tags with `print()`**

Using single or double quotation marks in `print()` statements can be useful when generating HTML tags that need double quotation marks, as in the following example.

```
print '<font color="blue">';
```

This above statement is easier to understand and actually runs slightly faster than using all double quotation marks and the backslash (\) character (to signal that the double quotation marks themselves should be output), as in the following example.

```
print "<font color=\"blue\">";
```

An Example Using the `rand()` and `print()` Functions

The following script shows an example of using `rand()` and `print()` (with single and double quotation marks). It uses a front-end HTML form that asks the user to pick the results of a coin flip. The form (shown at the top of Figure 4.1) uses the following radio buttons to ask the user for input.

```
<input type="radio" name="pick" value="0"> Heads
<input type="radio" name="pick" value="1"> Tails
```

The following script receives the input from the front-end form and decides whether the coin flip guess was correct. Lines 5 and 6 use the `srand()` and `rand()` functions to get a random number of either 0 or 1. The middle of Figure 4.1 shows the output when the user makes the wrong guess. The bottom of Figure 4.1 shows the output when the user makes a correct guess.

```
1.  <html>
2.  <head><title> Coin Flip Results </title></head>
3.  <body>
4.  <?php
5.      srand ((double) microtime() * 10000000);
6.      $flip = rand(0, 1);
7.
8.      if ( $flip == 0 && $pick == 0  ) {
9.          print "The flip=$flip, which is heads! <br> ";
10.         print '<font color="blue"> You got it right!</font>';
11.     } elseif ( $flip == 0 && $pick == 1  ) {
12.         print "The flip=$flip, which is heads! <br> ";
13.         print '<font color="red"> You got it wrong!</font>';
14.     } elseif ( $flip == 1 && $pick == 1  ) {
15.         print "The flip=$flip, which is tails! <br>";
16.         print '<font color="blue"> You got it right!</font>';
17.     } elseif ( $flip == 1 && $pick == 0  ) {
18.         print "The flip=$flip, which is tails! <br>";
19.         print '<font color="red"> You got it wrong!</font>';
20.         } else {
21.         print "<br>Illegal state error!";
22.     }
23.  ?>
24.  </body></html>
```

Check whether both the coin flip and the guess are heads.

Check whether the coin flip is heads but the guess is tails.

Check whether the coin flip is tails but the guess is heads.

Check whether both the coin flip and the guess are tails.

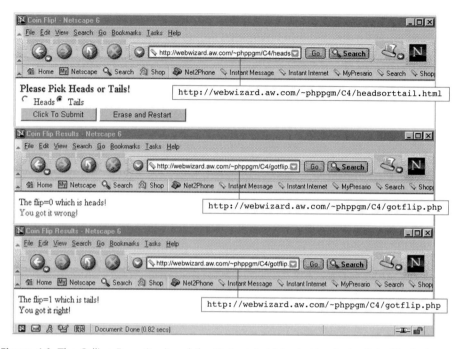

Figure 4.1 The Calling Form (top) and the Output (middle, bottom) of a Coin Flip Script

Here's a summary of the script's key lines.

☆ Lines 5–6 use the `srand()` and `rand()` functions to set `$flip` to a random number that is either 0 or 1.

☆ Lines 8–10 check whether the value of `$flip` is 0 and the value of `$pick` is 0. If so, the script outputs a message indicating that the flip was heads and that the user matched it. Note how line 10 uses single quotation marks in the `print` statement to enable it to output double quotation marks as part of the HTML output.

☆ Lines 11–13 check whether the value of `$flip` is 0 and the value of `$pick` is 1. If so, a message indicates that the flip was heads and that the user guessed incorrectly.

☆ Lines 14–16 check whether the value of `$flip` is 1 and the value of `$pick` is 1. If so, a message indicates that the flip was tails and that the user guessed correctly.

☆ Lines 17–19 check whether the value of `$flip` is 1 and the value of `$pick` is 0. If so, a message indicates that the flip was tails and that the user guessed incorrectly.

☆ Lines 20–22 check to see whether an erroneous input was received. If so, the script outputs an error message.

The date() Function

The `date()` function is a useful function for determining the current date and time (and a few other things). The `date()` function has the format shown in Figure 4.2.

> This string of one or more characters defines the output's format.

```
$x = date('format string');
```

> This variable receives date information in the requested format.

Figure 4.2 General Format of the `date()` Function

In Figure 4.2 you can see that the **format string** of one or more characters defines the format of the `date()` function's output. For example, a format string of `'d'` requests `date()` to return the current day of the month. Consider the following script segment.

```
$day = date('d');
print "day=$day";
```

> Request `date()` to return the numerical day of the month.

If the above script segment were carried out on December 27, 2001, then it would output "day=27".

Table 4.1 shows many of the format characters the `date()` function can use.

Table 4.1 Selected Character Formats for the `date()` Function

Format String	Meaning	Format String	Meaning
D	Three-letter indication of day of week (for example, Mon, Tue)	M	Current month of year in short three-letter format (for example, Jan, Feb)
d	Numerical day of month returned as two digits (for example, 01, 02)	s	Seconds in current minute from 00 to 59 (for example, 07, 50)
F	Current month in long format (for example, January, February)	t	Number of days in current month (28, 29, 30, or 31)
h	Current hour in day from 01 to 12 (for example, 02, 11)	U	Number of seconds since the epoch (usually since January 1, 1970)
H	Current hour in day from 00 to 23 (for example, 01, 18).	w	Current day of week from 0 to 6 (where 0 is Sunday, 1 is Monday, and so on)

(continues)

Table 4.1 Selected Character Formats for the date( ) Function *(continued)*

Format String	Meaning	Format String	Meaning
i	Current minute from 00 to 59 (for example, 05, 46)	y	Current year returned in two digits (for example, 01, 02)
l	Current day of week in long format (for example, Sunday, Monday)	Y	Current year returned in four digits (for example, 2001, 2002)
L	Returns 1 if it is a leap year or 0 otherwise	z	Day number of the year from 0 to 365 (where January 1 is day 0, January 2 is day 1, and so on)
m	Current month of year from 01 to 12		

You can combine multiple character formats to request the return of more than one format from the date( ) function. For example, on December 27, 2001, the script fragment below would output "Today=Thursday, December 27, 2001".

```
$today = date( 'l, F d, Y' );
print "Today=$today";
```

☆ TIP   Additional Options for the date() Function

Table 4.1 lists the most common date() options but not all the possible options. You can get more information on the date() function at http://www.php.net/date.

The following is an example of a Web application that uses date() to determine the current date and the number of days remaining in a store's sale event. Figure 4.3 shows the output of this script.

```
1.   <html>
2.   <head><title> Our Shop </title> </head>
3.   <body>
4.   <font size=4 color="blue">
5.   <?php
6.   $today = date( 'l, F d, Y' );
7.   print "Welcome on $today to our huge blowout sale! </font>";
8.   $month = date('m');
9.   $year = date('Y');
10.  $dayofyear = date('z');
11.  if ($month == 12 && $year == 2001) {
12.      $daysleft = (365 - $dayofyear + 10);
13.      print "<br> There are $daysleft sales days left";
```

> Check whether the month is 12 and the year is 2001.

```
14. } elseif ($month == 01 && $year == 2002) {
15.     if ($dayofyear <= 10) {
16.         $daysleft = (10 - $dayofyear);
17.         print "<br> There are $daysleft sales days left";
18.     } else {
19.         print "<br>Sorry, our sale is over.";
20.     }
21. } else {
22.     print "<br>Sorry, our sale is over.";
23. }
24. print "<br>Our Sale Ends January 10, 2002";
25. ?> </body></html>
```

> If the date is January 1, 2, 3, . . . 9, calculate the number of days remaining until January 10, 2002.

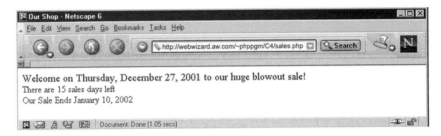

Figure 4.3 Output of the Sale Countdown Script

The following describes some of the key lines of the script.

☆ Line 6 gets the current day and date information and stores it in the variable `$today`.

☆ Lines 8–9 get the current month (in two-digit number format) and the current year (in four-digit format). Line 10 gets the numerical day of the year.

☆ Lines 11–13 determine whether the current month is December 2001. If so, it calculates the number of days remaining until the end of the year and adds 10 (for January 10, 2002).

☆ Lines 14–20 check to see if the current month is January 2002. If so, the script checks to see if the day is before or after January 10, 2002. If the date is before January 10, it calculates the number of remaining days in the sale. If the date is after January 10, the script prints a message that indicates the sale is over.

◎◎ Creating Your Own Functions

As you start to write more complex scripts, you will find it easier to understand and maintain your scripts if you divide them into logical sections. You might also find sets of statements carried out several times in different parts of a script.

Programmer-defined functions (also called **subroutines**) provide a way to group a set of statements, set them aside, and turn them into mini-scripts within a larger script. You can run these mini-scripts several times from different places in the overall script.

Using your own functions offers several advantages.

☆ *Smaller overall script size.* If a set of statements will be carried out more than once in the overall script, you can place these statements in a function and just call them when needed. This approach reduces the number of lines in the script. For example, if the script calculates a long, complex expression (perhaps a standard deviation) several times with different input values, placing the expression in a function will likely result in fewer lines of code.

☆ *Scripts that are easier to understand and change.* Functions can make complex and long scripts easier to understand and change. For example, consider a script that receives and verifies input from a Web form, queries a database, and generates a new Web page containing the result. Rather than writing this script as a long list of statements, you might use one function that reads and verifies input from a Web form, a second function that queries a database, and a third function that outputs the results to a Web page. With this logical division of tasks, the purpose of each section of code becomes much clearer.

☆ *Reusable script sections.* As you identify and define your own functions, you might find uses for some functions in other scripts. For example, you might define a function that creates a common page footer for Web pages on your site. You could place the function in an external file and then use this function in several different scripts that output Web pages for your site.

Working with Your Own Functions

You can create a function by placing a group of statements inside a function definition block, as shown in Figure 4.4.

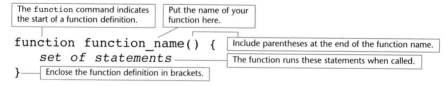

Figure 4.4 General Format of a Function Definition

Always start a function definition with the PHP reserved word `function`. Use your function name (indicated in Figure 4.4 by the placeholder `function_name`) to refer to the function later. The curly brackets (`{  .  .  .  }`) define a block of statements within the function. The set of statements consists of regular PHP statements that should run each time the function is called.

Suppose you want to create a function that automatically prints out the HTML tags needed to output two columns of a table. You might decide to create a function called `OutputTableRow()` that looks like the one below.

```
function OutputTableRow() {
    print '<tr><td>One</td><td>Two</td></tr>';
}
```

When you are ready to run this function within your script, enter the name of the function followed by parentheses.

```
OutputTableRow();
```

Whenever you call the `OutputTableRow()` function, the three lines of the `OutputTableRow()` function will be carried out. The following example shows a simple PHP script that uses the `OutputTableRow()` function. Figure 4.5 shows the script's output.

```
1.  <html>
2.  <head><title> Simple Table Function </title> </head> <body>
3.  <font color="blue" size="4"> Here Is a Simple Table <table border=1>
4.  <?php
5.      function OutputTableRow() {
6.          print '<tr><td>One</td><td>Two</td></tr>';
7.      }
8.      OutputTableRow();
9.      OutputTableRow();
10.     OutputTableRow();
11. ?>
12. </table></body></html>
```

Three consecutive calls to the `OutputTableRow()` function.

`OutputTableRow()` function definition.

http://webwizard.aw.com/~phppgm/C4/function1.php

Figure 4.5 Output of the `OutputTableRow()` Function

The list below summarizes the script.

☆ Line 3 creates the HTML to output some headline text and then sets `<table border=1>` to start the table.

☆ Lines 5–7 output a table row with two cells, with "One" in the first cell and "Two" in the second cell.

☆ Lines 8–10 call the function `OutputTableRow()` three times, each time outputting another row of the table.

☆**TIP** **Use Comments at the Start of a Function**

It is good practice to place comments at the start of a function to give a brief description of what the function does and perhaps how it is used. Recall that two slashes (//) precede a comment. The following example shows a simple comment at the beginning of a function definition.

```
function OutputTableRow() {
// Simple function that outputs 2 table cells
print '<tr><td>One</td><td>Two</td></tr>';
}
```

Passing Arguments to Functions

The example in Figure 4.5 has a major limitation: the function is not general enough. The function always outputs the same table row, with **"One"** in the first cell and **"Two"** in the second cell. To output different text in the cells, you have to change the function. One way to improve this function is to generalize it by allowing it to accept input variables for each table cell. These input variables are called **arguments to the function**.

☆**TIP** **You Have Already Used Arguments**

Several of the PHP functions introduced earlier in this book used arguments—such as the `abs()`, `rand()`, and `date()` functions. For example, `sqrt($num)` takes $num as an argument.

To send arguments to a function, place the arguments within parentheses when you call the function. Consider the following call to `OutputTableRow()`.

```
OutputTableRow("A First Cell", "A Second Cell");
```

This line calls `OutputTableRow()` with the first argument set to `"A First Cell"` and the second argument set to `"A Second Cell"`.

Within a function, you define the number and the names of the arguments in the first line of the function. For example, the following function receives two arguments, `$col1` and `$col2`. These arguments are output as part of a table row.

```
function OutputTableRow($col1, $col2) {
    print "<tr><td>$col1</td><td>$col2</td></tr>";
}
```

The following script uses the OutputTableRow( ) function as modified above. It uses a `for` loop to call the function four times, each with different argument values. Figure 4.6 shows the results.

```
1.   <html>
2.   <head><title> Simple Table Function </title> </head> <body>
3.   <font color="blue" size="4"> Revised Simple Table <table border=1>
4.   <?php
5.   function OutputTableRow( $col1, $col2 ) {
6.       print "<tr><td>$col1</td><td>$col2</td></tr>";
7.   }
8.       for ( $i=1; $i<=4; $i++ ) {
9.           $message1="Row $i Col 1";
10.          $message2="Row $i Col 2";
11.          OutputTableRow( $message1, $message2 );
12.      }
13.  ?>
14.  </table></body></html>
```

OutputTableRow( )
function definition.

Four calls to OuputTableRow( )
with different argument values.

Figure 4.6 Output of the OutputTableRow( ) Example with Arguments

Here's a summary of the script's key lines.

☆ Lines 5–7 create a new version of the OutputTableRow( ) function that uses the first ($col1) and second ($col2) arguments to determine the text to output for the first and second table cells, respectively, in the table row.

☆ Lines 8–12 create a `for` loop that repeats four times. Each loop calls OutputTableRow( ) with a different set of arguments.

☆**WARNING** **Make Sure You Send the Correct Number of Arguments**

Be sure that the number of arguments you define in the first line of a function matches the number of arguments you send to the function. If you send the wrong number of arguments, you may or may not get an error message, but you will likely get the wrong result.

Returning Values

You can define functions so that they return values to the calling script. For example, your functions can return the results of a computation. We already used return values with some of PHP's built-in functions. For example, the following code assigns the returned value of sqrt(144) to $result.

```
$result = sqrt(144);
```

Within a function, you can use the PHP return statement to return a value to the calling script statement. The return statement has the general format shown in Figure 4.7.

```
return $result;
```
This variable's value will be returned to the calling script.

Figure 4.7 General Format of the return Statement

The effect of the return statement is to stop the function and return the specified value to the calling script statement. As an example, the following code creates a simple function that compares two numbers and returns the larger of the values.

```
1. function Simple_calc($num1, $num2) {
2. // PURPOSE: returns largest of 2 numbers
3. // ARGUMENTS: $num1 -- 1st number, $num2 -- 2nd number
4.     if ($num1 > $num2) {
5.         return($num1);
6.     } else {
7.         return($num2);
8.     }
9. }
```
Return $num1 when it is the larger value.
Return $num2 if $num1 is not larger than $num2.

Here line 5 returns the first argument ($num1) if it is larger than $num2. Otherwise, line 7 returns the second argument ($num2).

If you call the Simple_calc() function as shown below, $largest will receive the returned value of 15.

```
$largest = Simple_calc(15, -22);
```

Now let's look at a complete script that calculates the percentage change from a starting value to an ending value and uses a function to return that percentage. The top of Figure 4.8 shows the calling form that requests the starting and ending values. This front-end form uses the following two key HTML lines, which define the text box form elements.

```
Starting Value: <input type="text" size="15"
                maxlength="20" name="start">
Ending Value: <input type="text" size="15"
                maxlength="20" name="end">
```

The middle of Figure 4.8 shows the output when the user enters a starting value of 80 and an ending value of 40. The bottom of Figure 4.8 shows the output when the user inputs the invalid values AAAA and BBBB.

```
1.   <html>
2.   <head><title> Your Percentage Calculation </title></head><body>
3.   <font color="blue" size="4"> Percentage Calculator </font>
4.   <?php
5.       function Calc_perc($buy, $sell) {
6.           $per = (($sell - $buy) / $buy) *100;
7.           return($per);
8.       }
9.       print "<br>Your starting value was $start.";
10.      print "<br>Your ending value was $end.";
11.      if (is_numeric($start) && is_numeric($end) ) {
12.          if ($start != 0) {
13.              $per = Calc_perc($start, $end);
14.              print "<br> Your percentage
                         change was $per %.";
15.          } else { print "<br> Error! Starting values cannot
                         be zero "; }
16.      } else { print "<br> Error! You must have valid numbers
                         for start and end "; }
17.  ?>
18.  </body></html>
```

Line 6 note: Calculate the percentage change from the starting value to the ending value.

Line 13 note: The call to `Calc_perc()` returns the percentage change into `$per`.

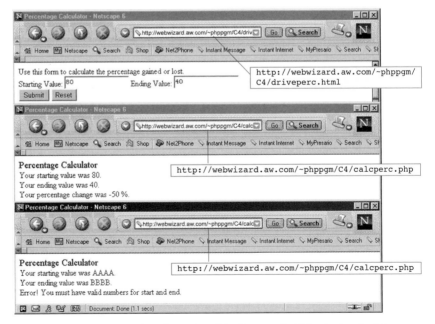

Figure 4.8 The Calling Form (top) and Two Possible Outputs (middle, bottom) of the Percentage Calculator Script

Here's a brief explanation of the script.

☆ Lines 5–8 define the function `Calc_perc()`, which receives two input values and returns the percentage change between the starting and ending values.

☆ Lines 11–12 determine whether the input values of `$start` and `$end` are valid numbers. Line 12 checks to ensure that `$start` is not zero to avoid the illegal mathematical operation of dividing by zero.

☆ Lines 13–14 call the `Calc_perc()` function with the input values `$start` and `$end` and then output the result. Note how `$per` receives the returned value of `Calc_perc()` in line 13.

☆ Lines 15–16 output error messages if the user inputs zero as the starting value or enters non-numeric values in the form.

☆ **SHORTCUT   Creating Functions with Optional Arguments**

You can create function definitions that use **optional arguments**. An optional argument does not need to be specified when the function is called. To create an optional argument, define a default value for the argument in the first line of the function definition. For example, consider the following function definition, which defines default values for the arguments `$size` and `$color`.

```
function OutputLine($text, $size = 3, $color = "black") {
    print "<font color=$color size=$size> $text </font>";
}
```

You can call the `OutputLine()` function with any of the following lines

```
OutputLine("Good Morning!");              // use size 3 and color "black"

OutputLine("Good Morning!", 4);    // use size 4 and color "black"

OutputLine("Good Morning!", 5, "red");     // use size 5 and color "red"
```

Changing Argument Values within a Function

Using a `return` statement works well when you have a single value to return to the calling script. Sometimes your functions may need to change more than one variable's value or need to pass results through its arguments. Normally, if a function changes a variable's value, that value is only known within that function. For example, the following code would not change the value of `$input` outside of the function and would therefore output "Inside input=12 Outside input=0".

```
function change_value($input) {
    $input = $input + 12;
    print "Inside input=$input ";
}
$input = 0;
change_value($input);
print " Outside input=$input";
```

> Change the value of `$input`.

> By default, changing a variable's value inside a function has no effect outside the function.

The value of `$input` is not changed in the main portion of the function since by default PHP passes the variable's *value* but not the actual variable. If you wish to pass the variable so it can be changed within the function, you must precede the variable name by an ampersand (`&`) in the calling statement (this is called *passing the variable by reference*). For example, the following code would change the value of `$input` in the main portion of the script and thus output "Inside input=17 Outside input=17":

```php
function change_value($input) {
    $input = $input + 12;
    print "Inside input=$input ";
}
$input = 5;
change_value(&$input);
print " Outside input=$input";
```

> Pass the actual variable by reference.

> Since $input was passed by reference, its value is changed.

Let's now look at an example that passes a variable to a function by reference and estimates the cost for a new carpet (including installation costs). It defines a function called `carpet_cost()` that receives as input the carpet width and length (in feet) and the carpet grade (best quality or extra value). The function calculates and sets values for the argument `$carpet_cost`. It will also return 0 if errors are found in the function's input arguments; otherwise, it will return 1. The top of Figure 4.9 shows the front-end form while the bottom shows the output of the following script.

```
1.   <html><head><title> Carpet Cost Quote </title> </head>
2.   <body> <font size="5" color="blue"> Your Estimated Carpet Costs </font>
3.   <?php
4.   function carpet_cost($width, $length, $grade, $carpet_cost) {
5.       if ($width > 0 && $length > 0) {
6.           if ($grade == 1) {
7.               $carpet_cost = $width * $length * 4.99;
8.               return 1;
9.           } elseif ($grade == 2) {
10.              $carpet_cost = $width * $length * 3.99;
11.              return 1;
12.          } else {
13.              print "Unknown carpet grade = $grade";
14.              return 0;
15.          }
16.      } else { return 0; }
17.  }
18.  $carpet_cost = 0; $install_cost = 0;
19.  $ret = carpet_cost($width, $length, $grade, &$carpet_cost);
20.  if ($ret) {
21.      $room_size = $width * $length;
22.      $total_cost = $carpet_cost + ($carpet_cost *.5);
23.      print "<br>Total square feet = $room_size";
```

> Return 0 if there is an error with the input arguments.

> Pass $carpet_cost by reference.

```
24.    print "<br>Carpet grade = $grade";
25.    print "<br>Carpet cost = \$$carpet_cost";
26.    print "<br>Total cost estimate (installed) = \$$total_cost";
27. } else { print "Illegal value received"; }
28. ?> </body></html>
```

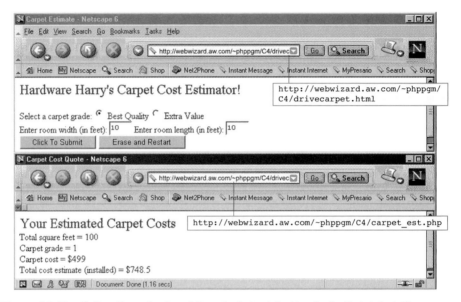

Figure 4.9 The Calling Form (top) and Sample Output (bottom) of a Script that Changes Input Arguments

Here's a summary of the key lines of the script.

☆ Line 4 is the start of the `carpet_cost()` function definition. It uses four input arguments: carpet width (`$width`), carpet length (`$length`), carpet grade (`$grade`), and carpet cost (`$carpet_cost`). The calculated carpet cost is returned through the `$carpet_cost` argument.

☆ Lines 5–16 check whether both `$length` and `$width` are greater than 0 and then calculate the carpet cost based on the carpet grade (`$grade` is received from the input form). If an error is found in the `$width`, `$length`, or `$grade`, the function returns a 0 value. Otherwise, the script sets `$carpet_cost` to the estimated carpet cost.

☆ Line 19 calls the `carpet_cost()` function with `$width`, `$length`, and `$grade` (set from the calling form) and `$carpet_cost` (passed by reference).

☆ Lines 20–27 check the return value from the `carpet_cost()` function and then output the total square feet, carpet grade, carpet cost, and estimated total carpet cost with installation. Line 22 calculates the total cost with carpet installation. (The installation cost is 50% of the carpet cost.)

Creating Your Own Functions

☆**WARNING Passing by Reference Is Generally Discouraged**

Scripts that pass many variables by reference to functions can be much harder to understand and debug than scripts that only pass variables by value. This is because passing variables by value limits variable changes to the inside of functions (other than when using a `return` statement). Most programmers try to design functions so they use minimal variables passed by reference.

Using External Script Files

Eventually, you will find some functions you develop could be useful to other PHP scripts. You might want to place these functions in separate files and reuse them in other scripts. For example, you might want to reuse the percentage calculation function `Calc_perc()`, from the script output in Figure 4.8, in other PHP scripts. Rather than entering the function in each script file, you can place it in a separate file and reuse it directly from this file. Being able to reuse functions helps speed up the development time of your scripts (especially when scripts get long). This can also make your scripts more modular, with smaller individual files, and thus easier to understand and debug.

PHP supports two different functions for including external script files in your scripts: `require()` and `include()`. They have the general formats shown in Figure 4.10.

The `require()` function produces a fatal error if it can't insert the specified file.

```
require  ("header.php");
include  ("trailer.php");
```

Both functions search for the file named within the double quotation marks and insert its PHP, HTML, or JavaScript code into the current file.

The `include()` function produces a warning if it can't insert the specified file.

Figure 4.10 General Format of the `require()` and `include()` Functions

Both functions search for the file specified within double quotation marks and insert its PHP, HTML, or JavaScript code into the current file. The difference is that the `require()` function produces a fatal error if it cannot find the external file. The `include()` function produces a warning message if it cannot find the external file.

As an example, suppose the file `header.php` contains the following lines of code.

```
1.   <font size="4" color="blue">
2.   Welcome to Harry's Hardware Heaven!
3.   </font><br> We sell it all for you!<br>
4.   <?php
5.   $time = date('H:i');
6.   function Calc_perc($buy, $sell) {
7.       $per = (($sell - $buy ) / $buy) * 100;
8.       return($per);
9.   }
10.  ?>
```

The script will output these lines when the file is included.

The value of $time will be set when the file is included.

This function will be available for use when the file is included.

If this file is included in a PHP script, it will output the HTML code in lines 1–3 and then run the PHP script in lines 4–10. Lines 4–10 will set the value of the variable $time to the current hour and minute (separated by a colon) and make the function Calc_perc() available. The following script includes the header.php file and uses the variable $time and the function Calc_perc() in its processing. The output of the script appears in Figure 4.11.

```
1.  <html><head><title> Hardware  Heaven </title></head> <body>
2.  <?php
3.      include("header.php");————[Include the file header.php.]
4.      $buy = 2.50;
5.      $sell = 10.00;
6.      print "<br>It is $time.";——[The value of $time is set in the header.php file.]
7.      print "We have hammers on special for \$$sell!";
8.      $markup = Calc_perc($buy, $sell);——[Calc_perc() is defined in the header.php file.]
9.      print "<br>Our markup is only $markup%!!";
10. ?>
11. </body></html>
```

Figure 4.11 Output of a Script Using the include() Function

Here's a brief explanation of the script.

☆ Lines 1–2 start the HTML document and PHP script.

☆ Line 3 uses the include() function to insert the code contained in the file header.php. The lines in this file output the first two lines in Figure 4.11, set a value for the variable $time, and then make the function Calc_perc() available.

☆ Lines 6–9 output the value of $time (set when the file header.php is included) and then use the Calc_perc() function. Finally, the script outputs the value returned from Calc_perc().

☆**TIP**   **More Typical Use of External Code Files**

The use of the `include()` function shown here is just an example. More typically you might use one or more files that contain only functions (for your PHP scripts to reuse) and other files that contain only HTML sections (for example, page headers or footers). In that way you could use the functions without needing to output HTML text. For example, if you want some common HTML text at the bottom of your pages, you can put the following HTML code into a file called `footer.php`.

```
<hr>
Hardware Harry's is located in beautiful downtown Hardwareville.
<br>We are open every day from 9 A.M. to midnight, 365 days a year.
<br>Call 476-123-4325. Just ask for Harry.
</body></html>
```

When you want to include this footer information in your HTML document, use the following line.

```
<?php include("footer.php"); ?>
```

☆ Summary

▷ PHP provides several functions useful for Web application development. The abs() function returns the absolute value of the number passed in. The round() function rounds the input number to the nearest integer. The is_numeric() function tests whether a variable contains a number or numeric string. The rand() function generates random numbers. The date() function can indicate the current day, month, year, and time.

▷ Programmer-defined functions allow you to group a set of statements, set them aside, and turn those grouped statements into mini-scripts within a larger script. You can run these mini-scripts several times from different places in the overall script. Programmer-defined functions help you create smaller scripts that are easier to understand, easier to modify, and reusable.

☆ Online References

PHP Function Quick Reference Guide
http://www.php.net/quickref.php

PHP Function Tutorial
http://www.phpbuilder.net/getit/functions.php3

A tutorial that describes how to build your own functions
http://www.zorka.com/index.php/phptutorial/

PHP overview and tutorial including discussion on building functions
http://hotwired.lycos.com/webmonkey/01/48/
index2a.html?tw=programming

☆ Review Questions

1. What would be the output of the following PHP script segment?

```
$x = sqrt(25); $y = round(12.4);
print "x=$x y=$y";
```

2. What would be the output of the following PHP script segment?

```
$x=1/3; $y = round( $x, 3 );
print 'The contents of $y ';
print "is $y";
```

3. What would be the output of the following PHP script segment?

```
srand ((double) microtime() * 10000000);
$numb = rand(1, 4);
print "numb=$numb";
```

4. What would be the output of the following PHP script segment?

```
$y=date("h:i:s");
print "y=$y";
```

5. What would be the output of the following PHP script segment?

```
$y=date("d:Y");
print "y=$y";
```

6. Name three advantages of writing your own functions.

7. Show the PHP code to create a function named `Output` that has one argument called `$outvar`. The function should output the argument using the `print` statement and then end.

8. What would be the output from the function `OutputTableRow()` (used for Figure 4.6) if it were called with each of the following statements?

   a. `OutputTableRow(1, 'Happy');`
   b. `OutputTableRow("Time", "OUT");`
   c. `OutputTableRow("Partial");`

9. What is an argument? Show a call to the `Calc_perc()` function (used for Figure 4.8) that would enable the function to change the value of `$buy`.

10. What would be the output of the following PHP code?

```
function change_value($input) {
    $input = $input * $input;
}
$input = 5;
change_value(&$input);
print "Answer=$input";
```

☆ Hands-On Exercises

1. Modify the front-end form and script from Figure 4.1 to have the user select the result of the roll of a single die (instead of a coin flip). Let the user know if he or she guessed the correct roll of the die.

2. Enhance the dice-guessing game from Exercise 1 by displaying an image of a die that matches the result of the die roll. Use six different pictures (available on the book's Web site). Hint: Use a common numerical suffix for each die image, such as `die1.gif`, `die2.gif`, `die3.gif`, and so on.

3. Create a simple Web page that lets the user know if your technical support office is open. If the day is Monday through Friday between 9 A.M. and 5 P.M., let the user know that the technical support department is open. Otherwise, let him or her know it is closed. Either way, output the current date and time.

4. Modify the script used for Figure 4.3 to create a Web page that notifies users of the number of days remaining in a *current* sale. Set the sale's end date to be the end of the current month. Correctly indicate when the sale is over and output how many days are left in the sale.

5. Create an application that calculates the total cost of a purchase. Include in the cost the item cost, shipping cost, and tax. Your Web application should have a front-end form requesting the user to enter the cost of a product. When the user submits the form, calculate the total cost (with shipping costs) of the product using the following guidelines.

   ✶ Add $3 if the product cost is less than or equal to $25.
   ✶ Add $4 if the product cost is $26–50.
   ✶ Add $5 if the product cost is $51–75.
   ✶ Add $6 if the product cost is more than $75.

   Use a function to calculate the shipping cost. Also, use a tax rate of 6% of the item cost (before adding in shipping costs).

6. Modify the script used for Figure 4.9 to calculate a different installation cost depending on the carpet grade. If the carpet grade is best quality, use an installation cost of 50% of the carpet cost. If the carpet grade is extra value, use an installation cost of 40% of the carpet cost. Calculate the installation costs as part of the `carpet_cost()` function.

CHAPTER FIVE

USING ARRAYS FOR LIST DATA

Sometimes it is handy to group related data values into a common list rather than to use a series of unrelated variables. Within PHP you can use a variable type called an array to store data in a list. PHP scripts that organize data into arrays can store and operate on the array data as a group. For example, you can use PHP functions to sort an array, search an array, or sum all array values. This chapter discusses how to use sequential and nonsequential arrays in PHP and describes some of the Web applications in which you can use them.

⊚◉ Chapter Objectives

☆ To understand the benefits of using arrays in PHP

☆ To learn how to create and use sequential arrays and their functions

☆ To learn how to create and use nonsequential arrays and their functions

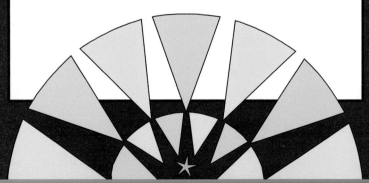

◎◉ Why Use Arrays?

PHP, like most other computer languages, offers a special variable type called a **list variable** or **array**. An array is a PHP variable that can hold multiple data values (like a list of numbers, names, or grocery items). A **sequential array** keeps track of these data items by using sequential numbers (for example, item 0, item 1, item 2, and so on). A nonsequential array or **associative array** keeps track of these data items by using character strings (for example, item meat, item poultry, item dairy, and so on).

Using arrays helps you organize data into a common list instead of working with separate variables. For example, instead of working with five variables called `$preference1`, `$preference2`, `$preference3`, `$preference4`, and `$preference5`, you might instead use one array variable that comprises a list of all five preference values. Organizing your data into one array variable enables your scripts to do tasks like the following.

☆ *Include a flexible number of list items.* Your scripts can add and delete items from arrays on the fly.

☆ *Examine each item more concisely.* You can use looping constructs (described in *Using Loops to Repeat Statements* in Chapter Three) in combination with arrays to look at and operate on each array item in a very concise manner.

☆ *Use special array operators and functions.* You can use PHP's built-in array operators and functions to do things such as count the number of items in your array, sum the data items, and sort your array.

Let's first look at defining and using sequential arrays and then examine associative arrays.

◎◉ Using Sequential Arrays

Creating Sequential Arrays

You can create an array by using the `array()` function. The `array()` function accepts a list of numerical or string values as arguments and returns an array created with the arguments. For example, if you want to store a set of four student names in an array, you can create an array called `$students[]` that specifies each student name, as shown in Figure 5.1.

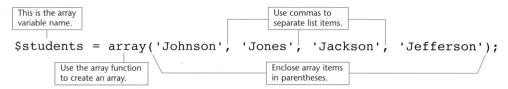

Figure 5.1 Using the `array()` Function to Create an Array

The statement in Figure 5.1 creates an array called `$students[]` with the string values `Johnson`, `Jones`, `Jackson`, and `Jefferson`. You can also create an array that comprises numerical data. For example, you could create an array of numerical items called `$grades[]` as follows:

```
$grades = array(66, 75, 85, 80);
```

This statement creates an array called `$grades[]` with the array items `66`, `75`, `85`, and `80`.

☆TIP Alternative Way to Create an Array

You can also create an array by making individual value assignments into the array variable name. For example, the following statements create the same array variable as the one created in Figure 5.1.

```
$students[] = 'Johnson';
$students[] = 'Jones';
$students[] = 'Jackson';
$students[] = 'Jefferson';
```

By default each of the above assignments adds the item to the *end* of the array.

Referencing Sequential Array Items

To reference individual array items, use an *array name* and *index pair*. The *index* (sometimes called a *subscript* or *key*) is always enclosed in square brackets (`[...]`). For example, the code line in Figure 5.2 uses the index `0` and an array variable named `$sports[]`.

```
$sports[0] = 'baseball';
```

Array name   Index

Figure 5.2 Referencing Individual Array Items

As you might imagine, in a sequential array indices are numbered sequentially, and by default index numbers start with 0 (not 1). So Figure 5.2 assigns `baseball` as the first item in the `$sports[]` array. As another example, consider the following PHP script segment.

```
$names = array('Denise', 'Christopher', 'Matthew', 'Bryant');
print ("$names[0], $names[1], $names[2], $names[3]");
```

The script segment would output "Denise, Christopher, Matthew, Bryant".

☆**WARNING Remember That Array Index Numbering Starts with 0**

You might think the arrays in the preceding code would be numbered with indices 1 through 4. Remember that by default sequential arrays start with index 0, so the indices above are numbered from 0 to 3. You must be careful in your scripts when accessing array items to avoid referencing an item past the end of your array (for example, using `$names[20]` in an array that contains only four items). Accessing these undefined items is not likely to produce desirable results in your scripts.

Array indices can be whole numbers or another variable. Consider the following example.

```
$i=3;
$classes = array('Math', 'History', 'Science', 'Pottery');
$oneclass = $classes[$i-1];
print "$classes[$i] $oneclass $classes[1] $classes[0]";
```

This code outputs the items in the `$classes[]` array in reverse order. That is, "Pottery Science History Math".

You can change values in an array variable and use them in expressions just as you would regular variables. Consider the example below.

```
$scores = array(75, 65, 85, 90);
$scores[3] = 95;
$average = ($scores[0] + $scores[1] +
            $scores[2] + $scores[3]) / 4;
print "average=$average";
```

The output of the above PHP segment is "average=80".

The first line in the above PHP segment creates an array variable called `$scores[]` with the initial values 75, 65, 85, and 90. The second line reassigns the fourth array item from 90 to 95 (remember that numbering goes from 0 to 3, not from 1 to 4). The third line sets `$average` equal to `(75 + 65 + 85 + 95) / 4`—that is, to 80.

If you wish, you can explicitly set index values for your array. The following example uses the PHP `=>` operator to explicitly assign the indices 1, 2, and 3 to values in the `array()` function.

Add item with value 100 to the end of the array.

Assign the value of 75 to the item with index 1.

Assign the value of 65 to the item with index 2.

Assign the value of 85 to the item with index 3.

```
$scores = array(1=>75, 2=>65, 3=>85);
$scores[] = 100;
print "$scores[1] $scores[2] $scores[3] $scores[4]";
```

The above script segment outputs "75 65 85 100".

Note how PHP automatically assigns the item to the next sequential index value when no index is specified in the second line.

Using Loops with Sequential Arrays

Looping statements are often used with sequential arrays as a way to iterate through array items. For example, the following script segment loops through each item of the `$courses[]` array. It uses the PHP `count()` function to return the number of items currently in the array.

```
$courses = array ('Perl', 'PHP', 'C',
           'Java', 'Pascal', 'Cobol', 'Visual Basic');
for ($i=0; $i < count($courses); $i++) {
   print ("$courses[$i] ");
}
```

The above `for` loop repeats seven times with the value of `$i` changing from 0 to 1, 2, 3, 4, 5, and then 6. Therefore, the output of this script segment is "Perl PHP C Java Pascal Cobol Visual Basic".

Another way to access each array item in a loop is to use the special `foreach` loop construct, which follows the general format shown in Figure 5.3.

Specify the name of the array to use in the loop.	This variable is automatically set to the next array item each iteration.

```
foreach ($courses as $item) {
   Set of statements to repeat.
}
```

Figure 5.3 General Format of the `foreach` Command

The `foreach` loop shown in Figure 5.3 automatically assigns the variable `$item` a different item from `$courses[]` in each loop iteration. As an example, consider the following script segment.

```
$courses = array('Perl', 'PHP', 'C', 'Java', 'Pascal',
                'Cobol', 'Visual Basic');
foreach ($courses as $item){
   print ("$item ");
}
```

This script segment outputs "Perl PHP C Java Pascal Cobol Visual Basic".

The following full PHP script example uses an array (defined in line 6) to maintain a list of menu items. These items are output via a `for` loop (lines 9–15) that creates a set of radio buttons. (The user is asked to select his or her favorite items from the Tuna Café.) Note that an advantage of using a menu array is that if the café's menu changes, the menu items can be easily added and deleted by just changing line 6. Note also that line 10 creates a check box using `name="prefer[]"`, which will enable the receiving script (at `http://webwizard.aw.com/~phppgm/C5/tunaresults.php`) to receive multiple checklist items. The top of Figure 5.4 shows the output of the script shown below.

```
1.   <html><head><title> Tuna Cafe </title></head>
2.   <body> <font size="4" color="blue">
3.   Welcome to the Tuna Cafe Survey! </font>
4.   <form action="http://webwizard.aw.com/~phppgm/C5/
            tunaresults.php" method=post>
5.   <?php
6.   $menu = array('Tuna Casserole', 'Tuna Sandwich',
                'Tuna Pie', 'Grilled Tuna', 'Tuna Surprise');
7.   $bestseller = 2;
8.   print 'Please indicate all your favorite dishes.<br>';
9.   for ($i=0; $i < count($menu); $i++) {
10.     print "<input type=\"checkbox\" name=\"prefer[]\"
                value=$i> $menu[$i]";
11.     if ($i == $bestseller) {
12.        print '<font color="red"> Our Best Seller!!!! </font>';
13.     }
14.     print '<br>';
15.  }
16.  ?>
17.  <input type="submit" value="Click To Submit">
18.  <input type="reset" value="Erase and Restart">
19.  </form></body></html>
```

Create a list of menu items.

This array will be available to the receiving script when the form is submitted.

Here's a summary of the script's key lines.

☆ Line 6 defines the list of items in the $menu[ ] array.

☆ Line 7 sets the $bestseller variable with value 2. Lines 11–12 use this value to output an additional message for the third item of the $menu[ ] array.

☆ Lines 9–15 loop through each menu item in the array and create a check box form element. When the value of $i is equal to $bestseller, an additional message is output indicating the best-selling item (lines 11–13). Note that line 10 uses prefer[ ] in the name argument of the check box form element. This enables passing an array of selections to the receiving script. (See the next section for details on receiving an array of selections.)

Using Arrays to Receive Multiple Form Element Selections

We discussed in Chapter Two that checklists and selection lists can send more than one value for a variable of a form element. In the previous script (with output shown at the top of Figure 5.4), line 10 sets the variable prefer[ ] to hold a list of check box values selected by the user:

```
print "<input type=\"checkbox\" name=\"prefer[]\"
            value=$i> $menu[$i]";
```

Within the receiving PHP script (at http://webwizard.aw.com/~phppgm/C5/tunaresults.php), the variable $prefer[ ] is an array that holds each check box item selected. For example, if the user selects the first and third check box items shown at the top of Figure 5.4, then $prefer[ ] would be an array of two items: the first item, $prefer[0], would have a value of 0, and the second item, $prefer[1], would have a value of 2.

As a more complete example, consider the following script, which processes the form shown in at the top of Figure 5.4. The script below checks to ensure that the user selected at least one item, and if so, it creates an HTML document with each of the selected items in a bullet list. It uses the same array (line 6) as set in the previous script that generates the front-end form (shown at the top of Figure 5.4). The output of this script is shown in at the bottom of Figure 5.4.

```
1.  <html>
2.  <head><title> Tuna Cafe </title></head>
3.  <body>
4.  <font size="4" color="blue"> Tuna Cafe Results Received </font>
5.  <?php
6.      $menu = array('Tuna Casserole', 'Tuna Sandwich',
                      'Tuna Pie', 'Grilled Tuna', 'Tuna Surprise');
7.      if (count($prefer) == 0 ) {    ── If $prefer[ ] is empty, the user didn't select any items.
8.          print 'Oh no! Please pick something as your favorite! ';
9.      } else {
10.         print '<br>Your selections were <ul>';
11.         foreach ($prefer as $item) {        ──── Loop through the
12.             print "<li>$menu[$item]</li>";   ──── $prefer[ ] array
13.         }                                         and output selected
14.         print '</ul>';                            items as an HTML
15.     }                                             bullet list.
16. ?>
17. </body></html>
```

Let's review some of the key lines of the script.

☆ Line 6 creates the $menu[ ] array to hold a list of menu items. It uses the same array definition as the front-end script shown at the top of Figure 5.4.

☆ Lines 7–8 check the number of items in the $prefer[ ] array. If there are no items in the array, the script outputs an error message.

☆ Lines 11–13 use a foreach loop to iterate through the items of the $prefer[ ] array. During each iteration of the loop, the value of $item is used as an index to the $menu[ ] array to output the items selected by the user.

☆ TIP   **This Script Should Be More Defensive**

The script for Figure 5.4 should be more careful to ensure that the items of the $prefer[ ] array are valid numbers and have valid values. You should use care whenever you receive input from a user. Remember that there are different ways to start and send input to your scripts. For example, someone may access your script with his or her own form instead of the one you designed. They may use such a form to intentionally or unintentionally set incorrect input values.

Figure 5.4 Receiving Multiple Checklist Items into a PHP Script

Adding and Deleting Items

Sometimes your Web application may need to add and remove items from an array. PHP supports a set of four different functions—`array_shift()`, `array_unshift()`, `array_pop()`, and `array_push()`—that can add items to and remove items from the beginning and end of an array (Figure 5.5). The following section describes these four functions.

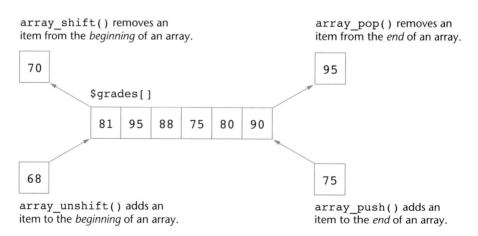

array_shift() removes an item from the *beginning* of an array.

array_pop() removes an item from the *end* of an array.

array_unshift() adds an item to the *beginning* of an array.

array_push() adds an item to the *end* of an array.

Figure 5.5 The Effects of the `array_shift()`, `array_unshift()`, `array_pop()`, and `array_push()` Functions

The `array_shift()` and `array_unshift()` Functions

These two functions respectively remove items from and add items to the *beginning* of an array. The `array_shift()` function accepts an array variable as an argument, removes the first item, and then returns the removed item. For example, the following code outputs "Day off = Monday Work week = Wednesday Friday".

This item was removed.

```
$work_week = array('Monday', 'Wednesday', 'Friday');
$day_off = array_shift($work_week);
print "Day off = $day_off Work week = ";
foreach ($work_week as $day) {
    print "$day ";
}
```

The counterpart to `array_shift()` is the `array_unshift()` function, used to *add* an item to the *beginning* of the array. It accepts as arguments an array variable and an item to add. For example, the following code outputs "Work week is now = Sunday Monday Wednesday Friday".

This item was added.

```
$work_week = array('Monday', 'Wednesday','Friday');
array_unshift($work_week, 'Sunday');
print 'Work week is now = ';
foreach ($work_week as $day) {
    print "$day ";
}
```

The `array_pop()` and `array_push()` Functions

These two functions respectively remove items from and add items to the *end* of an array. The `array_pop()` function accepts an array variable as an argument and returns an item it removed from the end of the array. For example, the following code outputs "Day off = Friday Work week = Monday Wednesday".

This item was removed.

```
$work_week = array('Monday', 'Wednesday', 'Friday');
$day_off = array_pop($work_week);
print "Day off = $day_off Work week = ";
foreach ($work_week as $day) {
    print "$day ";
}
```

The counterpart to `array_pop()` is `array_push()`. This function accepts an array variable and an item as arguments and adds the item to the end of an array. For example, the following code outputs "Work week is now = Monday Wednesday Friday Saturday".

This item was added.

```
$work_week = array('Monday', 'Wednesday','Friday');
array_push($work_week, 'Saturday');
print 'Work week is now = ';
foreach ($work_week as $day) {
    print "$day ";
}
```

⭐ **SHORTCUT** **Removing an Item from an Array**

You can use `array_shift()` and `array_pop()` to remove items from the front and back of an array, respectively, without saving the results into a variable. For example, the following code removes an item from the end of the $work_week variable.

```
array_pop($work_week);
```

Additional Useful Array Functions

PHP has several additional functions useful for working with sequential arrays. You can use these functions to determine maximum and minimum array values, to sum all numerical array items, and to sort an array among other things.

The max() and min() Functions

Use these functions to determine the largest and smallest numerical values in an array. Each function accepts an array as an input argument and returns either the maximum or minimum numerical value in the array. For example, the following script segment outputs "max=100 small=16".

```
$grades = array (99, 100, 55, 91, 65, 22, 16);
$big=max($grades);
$small=min($grades);
print "max=$big small=$small";
```

The array_sum() Function

Use this function to sum all the *numerical* values in an array. The `array_sum()` function accepts an array as an argument and returns the summation of all its *numerical* values. For example, the following script segment outputs "Total=175".

```
$grades = array (25, 100, 50, 'N/A');
$total=array_sum($grades);
print "Total=$total";
```

The sort() Function

Use this function to reorder an array in alphabetical or numerical order. Sorting the values of a sequential array can be useful in a variety of tasks. For example, you might want to output student grades sorted from highest to lowest or output a set of names sorted alphabetically. The `sort()` function accepts an array as an argument and then sorts that array. For example, the following code segment outputs

☆**WARNING** **Mixing Character and Numerical Variable Types**

PHP will try to convert character variables to numerical values when it can to complete the requested function or operation. For example, examine the following PHP code.

```php
<?php
$grades = array ('2 nights', '3days', 50, '1 more day');
$total=array_sum($grades);
print "total=$total";
?>
```

Instead of generating an error message, this code outputs "total=56".

"C Cobol Java PHP Pascal Perl Visual Basic". Note that the string `"PHP"` sorts before the string `"Pascal"` because ASCII upper case characters have lower ASCII code values than lower case.

```php
$courses = array ('Perl', 'PHP', 'C',
            'Java', 'Pascal', 'Cobol', 'Visual Basic');
sort($courses);
foreach ($courses as $course) {
    print " $course ";
}
```

The `sort()` function can also sort numerical data. For example, the following code segment outputs "1 11 55 91 99 119 911".

```php
$courses = array (91, 55, 11, 1, 99, 911, 119);
sort($courses);
foreach ($courses as $item) {
    print "$item ";
}
```

☆**SHORTCUT** **Additional Array Functions**

PHP supports many other array functions that can reverse the order of an array, output the differences between two arrays, search an array for an item, and even sort an array in reverse order (largest value first). You can find more information at `http://www.php.net/array`.

◎◎ Using Associative Arrays

Creating Associative Arrays

So far, the arrays we have created all use sequential numerical indices (for example, `preference[0]`, `$preference[1]`, `$preference[2]`, and so on). PHP also supports using string-value indices to create **associative arrays**. Associative arrays index data values by a character string instead of a numerical value. The string-value index is used to look up or provide a cross-reference to the data value. For example, the following code creates an associative array with three items.

```
$instructor['Science'] = 'Smith';
$instructor['Math'] = 'Jones';
$instructor['English'] = 'Jackson';
```

Using string-value indices for arrays make it possible to cross-reference one piece of data with another. For example, you may have an associative array that cross-references *states* with *capitals*, *names* with *grades*, or *part numbers* with corresponding *part descriptions*.

You can create associative arrays (with string-value indices) by using the `array()` function in the general format shown in Figure 5.6. In this example, the variable $months is the name of the associative array. Notice how the items are assigned in index/value pairs using the PHP => operator. For example, `'Jan'` is an index with a value of 31, `'Feb'` is an index with a value of 28, `'Mar'` is an index with a value of 31, and so on.

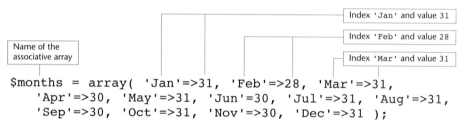

```
$months = array( 'Jan'=>31, 'Feb'=>28, 'Mar'=>31,
    'Apr'=>30, 'May'=>31, 'Jun'=30, 'Jul'=>31, 'Aug'=>31,
    'Sep'=>30, 'Oct'=>31, 'Nov'=>30, 'Dec'=>31 );
```

Figure 5.6 Using the `array()` Function to Create a PHP Associative Array

Accessing Associative Array Items

When you want to access an item in an associative array, use a syntax similar to the one used for sequential arrays, but use a string value or variable for the index (Figure 5.7).

Enclose the index in square brackets.

```
$days = $months['Mar'];
```

This variable receives the data value associated with 'Mar'.   Use a string value for the index.

Figure 5.7 Accessing Items in an Associative Array

☆**WARNING** **You Cannot Fetch Indices by Using Data Values**

You might be tempted to use a data item to fetch an index from an associative array, as in the following example:

```
$mon = $months[28];
```

This syntax is incorrect because associative arrays can fetch data values only by using indices (not the other way around).

The following example uses an associative array and calculates the distance from Chicago, Illinois, to various cities in the United States. The front-end HTML form appears at the top of Figure 5.8. It uses the following select list form element.

This sets $destination in the form-processing script.

```
<select name="destination" size="3">
<option> Boston </option>
<option> Dallas </option>
<option> Las Vegas </option>
<option> Miami </option>
<option> Nashville </option>
<option> Pittsburgh </option>
<option> San Francisco </option>
<option> Toronto </option>
<option> Washington, DC </option>
</select>
```

When the user selects a city and submits the form, the form-processing script uses an associative array to look up the distance between Chicago, Illinois and the destination city received in $destination. It also calculates the driving time (distance divided by 60) and the walking time (distance divided by 5). Note how line 6 uses the isset() function to check if the destination city has a value in the associative array. The output from this script is shown at the bottom of Figure 5.8.

Associative array containing destination city and distance.

Check if the input destination city has a value in $cities[].

Round results to 2 digits to the right of the decimal point.

```
1.  <html>
2.  <head><title> Distance and Time Calculations </title></head>
3.  <body>
4.  <?php
5.  $cities = array ('Dallas' => 803, 'Toronto' => 435,
            'Boston' => 848, 'Nashville' => 406,
            'Las Vegas' => 1526, 'San Francisco' => 1835,
            'Washington, DC'=> 595, 'Miami' => 1189,
            'Pittsburgh' => 409);
6.  if (isset($cities[$destination])) {
7.      $distance = $cities[$destination];
8.      $time = round( ($distance / 60), 2);
9.      $walktime = round( ($distance / 5), 2);
10.     print "The distance between Chicago and <i>
            $destination</i> is $distance miles.";
11.     print "<br>Driving at 60 miles per hour it would take
            $time hours.";
12.     print "<br>Walking at 5 miles per hour it would take
            $walktime hours.";
13. } else {
14.     print "Sorry, do not have destination information for
            $destination.";
15. } ?>
16. </body></html>
```

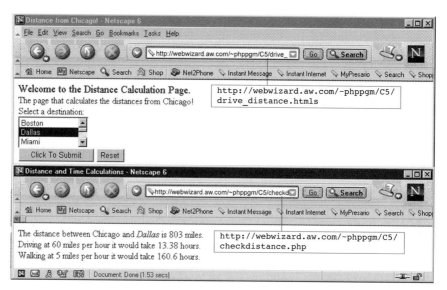

Figure 5.8 HTML Input Form (top) and Sample Output (bottom) of a Script That Calculates the Distance and Travel Times from Chicago to Selected Cities

Here's a summary of this script.

☆ Line 5 defines an associative array (called `$cities[]`) that uses city names as array indices and total miles from Chicago as array values.

☆ Line 6 uses the `isset()` function to determine whether the input destination city (from the calling form) has a value in the `$cities` associative array. (More details on using `isset()` with an associative array are provided below in the *Changing, Adding, Deleting, and Verifying Associative Array Items* section.)

☆ Lines 7–9 first get the total distance (in miles) to the destination city from Chicago by using the values in the `$cities` associative array. Then these lines calculate the total driving time (by dividing the distance by 60 miles per hour) and walking time (by dividing the distance by 5 miles per hour). The `round()` function is used to round the results of these calculations to two digits after the decimal point.

☆ Lines 10–12 output the distance to the destination city and the driving and walking times.

☆ Line 14 is output when the script receives an input in `$destination` that does not exist in the `$cities` associative array. Such input is not expected but could occur if the user submits input arguments via some other input form or via the URL.

Using Loops with Associative Arrays

As with sequential arrays, you can use the `foreach` loop to iterate through items in an associative array. Use a `foreach` loop in the general format shown in Figure 5.9 to access both the array indices and items.

Specify the name of the array to use in the loop.

```
foreach ($courses as $index => $item) {
    Set of statements to repeat
}
```

Index variable ($index) is automatically set to next array index each iteration.

Item variable ($item) is automatically set to next array value each iteration.

Figure 5.9 General Format of the `foreach` Command for Accessing Associative Array Indices and Values

As you can see in Figure 5.9, when using a `foreach` loop you can specify an array name, an index variable, and an array item variable. The `foreach` loop automatically assigns the *index variable* and *item variable* (`$index` and `$item` in Figure 5.9) a different array index and value for each loop iteration. As an example, consider the following script segment.

```
$inventory = array('Nuts'=>33, 'Bolts'=>55, 'Screws'=>12);
foreach ($inventory as $index => $item) {
    print "Index is $index, value is $item<br> ";
}
```

This script segment outputs the following lines.

```
Index is Nuts, value is 33
Index is Bolts, value is 55
Index is Screws, value is 12
```

Changing, Adding, Deleting, and Verifying Associative Array Items

Now that you have seen how to create and output an associative array, let's focus on how to change, add, delete, and verify the existence of associative array items.

Changing an Associative Array Value

You can change the value of an associative array item by giving it a new value in an assignment statement. Here's an example.

```
$inventory = array('Nuts'=> 33, 'Bolts'=> 55, 'Screws'=> 12);
$inventory['Nuts'] = 100;
```

The second line changes the value associated with `Nuts` to `100`.

Adding an Associative Array Item

You can add items to an associative array by assigning a value to a new index name, as shown below.

```
$inventory = array('Nuts'=>33, 'Bolts'=>55, 'Screws'=>12);
$inventory['Nails'] = 23;
```

The second line adds an array item with index `'Nails'` and a value of 23 to the associative array.

Deleting an Associative Array Item

You can delete an item from an associative array by using the `unset()` function. Here's an example.

```
$inventory = array('Nuts'=> 33, 'Bolts'=>55, 'Screws'=> 12);
unset($inventory['Nuts']);
```

The second line deletes the array item with index `'Nuts'` and a value of 33 from the associative array.

Verifying an Item's Existence

You can use the `isset()` function to verify whether a particular index exists in the associative array. It returns *true* if the index passed as an argument appears in the associative array. It returns *false* if the index is not in the array. The following example demonstrates the use of the `isset()` function.

```
$inventory = array('Nuts'=> 33, 'Bolts'=>55, 'Screws'=> 12);
if  (isset($inventory['Nuts'])) {
    print ('Nuts are in the list.');
} else {
    print ('No Nuts in this list.');
}
```

This code outputs "Nuts are in the list."

☆TIP   **Changing Index Values**

You can change the value of an existing index but you cannot change or rename an index for a particular value in the associative array. The best way to accomplish the latter goal is to delete the index/value pair and then add the new index and value.

☆WARNING   **Indices Are Case-Sensitive**

Like many things in PHP, indices are case-sensitive. Thus, if you wrote the following two lines, you would end up with an array with four items with the indices `'Nuts'`, `'Bolts'`, `'Screws'`, and `'nuts'` and would not change the value stored with index `'Nuts'`.

```
$inventory = array( 'Nuts'=> 33, 'Bolts'=>55, 'Screws'=>12 );
$inventory['nuts'] = 32;
```

The following example illustrates some of the array operations we just discussed. The script enables the user to add an item to an associative array from an input form (shown at the top of Figure 5.10). The input HTML form uses the following key lines.

```
<input type="radio" name="Action" value="Add" > Add
<input type="radio" name="Action" value="Unknown" > Unknown
<br>Enter Index: <input type="text" name="index" size="10">
Enter Value: <input type="text" name="Value" size="10">
```

The bottom screen of Figure 5.10 shows the output when the following script is carried out. Note how this script uses the `isset()` function (in line 7) to check whether the index exists before trying to add it to the associative array.

```
1.   <html><head><title>Inventory Add </title>
2.   </head><body>
3.   <?php
4.   $invent = array('Nuts'=>44, 'Nails'=>34, 'Bolts'=>31);
5.   if ($Action == 'Add'){———————[ Check whether the user selected the Add operation as input. ]
6.       $item=$invent["$index"];                    [ Use isset() to check whether the
7.       if (isset($invent["$index"])) {———————  index exists in the associative array. ]
8.           print "Sorry, already exists $index <br>";
9.       } else {
10.          $invent["$index"] = $Value;
11.          print "Adding index=$index value=$Value <br>";
12.          print '-----<br>';
13.          foreach ($invent as $index => $item) {
14.              print "Index is $index, value is $item.<br> ";
15.          }
16.      }
17.  } else { print "Sorry, no such action=$Action<br>"; }
18.  ?></body></html>
```

Here's a summary of the key lines of this script.

☆ Line 4 creates an associative array of three items with the indices `'Nuts'`, `'Nails'`, and `'Bolts'`.

☆ Line 5 uses the checks if the `$Action` input variable is equal to `'Add'`.

☆ Line 7 uses the `isset()` function to check whether the index input from the front-end form has a value in the associative array.

☆ Lines 10–16 run if the index does not already have a value in the associative array. Line 10 adds the index/value pair to the list, and lines 13–15 output the entire array.

☆ Line 17 outputs an error message if the `$Action` variable is not equal to `'Add'`.

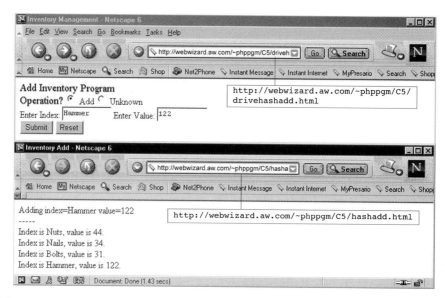

Figure 5.10 HTML Input Form (top) and Sample Output (bottom) of a Script That Adds an Item to an Associative Array

Sorting Associative Arrays

PHP supports a special set of functions for sorting associative arrays.

The `asort()` Function

Use this function to sort an associative array and maintain the relationship between the indices and values. The `asort()` function takes an associative array as an argument and then sorts it using the associative array *values* as a sort field. For example, the following script segment outputs "Nashville = 406 Toronto = 435 Dallas = 803 Boston = 848 Las Vegas = 1526".

```
$dest = array('Dallas' => 803, 'Toronto' => 435,
              'Boston' => 848, 'Nashville' => 406,
              'Las Vegas' => 1526);
   asort($dest);
   foreach ($dest as $index => $value) {
      print " $index = $value ";
}
```

The `ksort()` Function

This function is similar to the `asort()` function but it sorts an associative array using the *indices* as the sort field. For example, the following segment outputs "Boston = 848 Dallas = 803 Las Vegas = 1526 Nashville = 406 Toronto = 435".

```
$dest = array ('Dallas' => 803, 'Toronto' => 435,
               'Boston' => 848, 'Nashville' => 406,
               'Las Vegas' => 1526);
ksort($dest);
foreach ($dest as $index => $value) {
    print " $index = $value ";
}
```

Using Multidimensional Arrays

Some data are best represented by creating a list of lists (sometimes called a **multidimensional array**). For example, you could represent the data in Table 5.1 (which lists four different inventory parts, each with a part name, count, and price) as a multidimensional associative array, as shown in Figure 5.11.

Table 5.1 Sample Data to Be Represented with a Multidimensional Array

Part Number	Part Name	Count	Price
AC1000	Hammer	122	12.50
AC1001	Wrench	5	5.00
AC1002	Handsaw	10	10.00
AC1003	Screwdriver	222	3.00

Specify the name of the multidimensional array.

Each item has an index and a value.

```
$inventory = array (
    'AC1000'=>array('Part'=>'Hammer','Count'=>122, 'Price'=>12.50),
    'AC1001'=>array('Part'=>'Wrench','Count'=>5, 'Price'=>5.00),
    'AC1002'=>array('Part'=>'Handsaw','Count'=>10, 'Price'=>10.00),
    'AC1003'=>array('Part'=>'Screwdriver','Count'=>222, 'Price'=>3.00)
);
```

This line defines part number 'AC1003' as an index to a list of items that include a 'Part', 'Count', and 'Price'.

Enclose each row in parentheses and end each row (except the last one) in a comma.

Figure 5.11 Example of a Statement That Creates a Multidimensional Associative Array

The code from Figure 5.11 creates a multidimensional associative array that uses 'AC1000', 'AC1001', 'AC1002', and 'AC1003' as indices. The value of each index is another associative array that uses 'Part', 'Count', and 'Price' as indices. For example, 'AC1000' is an index to an associative array that uses 'Part', 'Count', and 'Price' as indices with values Hammer, 122, and 12.50.

You can access items from the above multidimensional array much as you would access items from an associative array, except you must add an *additional* index to identify a specific item in the multidimensional array. For example, using the multidimensional array defined in Figure 5.11, `$inventory['AC1000']['Part']` has the value Hammer, `$inventory['AC1001']['Count']` has the value 5, and `$inventory['AC1002']['Price']` has the value 10.00.

You can change and access individual items in a multidimensional associative array as you would with regular associative arrays. For example, the following code uses the `$inventory` multidimensional associative array defined in Figure 5.11 and adds 1 to its 'Count' value.

```
$inventory['AC1001']['Count'] = $inventory['AC1001']['Count'] + 1;
$partName=$inventory['AC1001']['Part'];
print "$partName, has {$inventory['AC1001']['Count']} items";
```

> You must use curly brackets when you output a multidimensional array item in a print statement.

This code outputs the following: "Wrench, has 6 items". Note that PHP requires the use of curly brackets ({ . . . }) around a multidimensional item in a `print` statement.

The next full PHP script demonstrates how to access items in a multidimensional array. It uses a front-end HTML form (shown at the top of Figure 5.12) that requests the user to select a part number. This HTML form uses the following radio button form elements.

```
<input type="radio" name="id" value="AC1000"> AC1000
<input type="radio" name="id" value="AC1001"> AC1001
<input type="radio" name="id" value="AC1002"> AC1002
<input type="radio" name="id" value="AC1003"> AC1003
```

When the user submits the form, the following PHP script (at http://webwizard.aw.com/~phppgm/C5/show_inventory.php) outputs a part name, an inventory count, and a price for the input part ID. Note how line 4 in the script below defines a multidimensional associative array. Also note how the `isset()` function is used in line 5 to check whether the `$id` variable has a valid value in the array. The bottom of Figure 5.12 shows the output of the following script.

```
1.   <html><head><title>Inventory Information</title>
2.   </head><body>
3.   <?php
4.   $inventory = array (
         'AC1000'=>array('Part'=>'Hammer','Count'=>122,
                         'Price'=> 12.50 ),
         'AC1001' =>array('Part' =>'Wrench','Count' =>5,
                         'Price'=>5.00 ),
         'AC1002'=>array('Part' =>'Handsaw','Count' =>10,
                         'Price'=>10.00 ),
         'AC1003'=>array('Part' =>'Screwdrivers',
                         'Count'=>222, 'Price'=>3.00)
     );
```

> Define the same multidimensional array used in Figure 5.11.

```
5.   if (isset($inventory[$id])){
6.       print '<font size="4" color="blue"> ';
7.       print "Inventory Information for Part $id </font>";
8.       print '<table border=1> <th> ID <th> Part <th> Count
             <th> Price ';
9.       print "<tr> <td> $id </td>";
10.      print "<td> {$inventory[$id]['Part']} </td>";
11.      print "<td> {$inventory[$id]['Count']} </td>";
12.      print "<td> \${$inventory[$id]['Price']} </td></tr>";
13.  } else {
14.      print "Illegal part ID = $id ";
15.  }
16.  ?> </body></html>
```

> Output specific items form
> the multidimensional array.

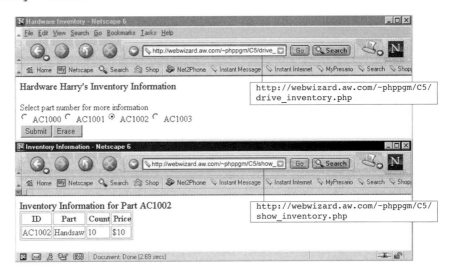

Figure 5.12 HTML Input Form (top) and Sample Output (bottom) for a Script That Uses a Multidimensional Array in a Form

Here's a summary of this script.

☆ Line 4 defines `$inventory`, a multidimensional associative array of inventory items.

☆ Line 5 uses `isset()` to check whether `$id` (received as input from the calling form) has a value in the multidimensional array. If not, the user sent an illegal `$id` value to the script.

☆ Lines 6–12 output information about the part number in a table format. Note how lines 10–12 use curly brackets when printing a multidimensional array item. Note also how line 12 prints a dollar sign by first using a backslash (\).

☆ Line 14 prints out an error message when an illegal `$id` value is received in the script. This message might output if the user fails to make a part number selection from the front-end form or runs the script from a different form.

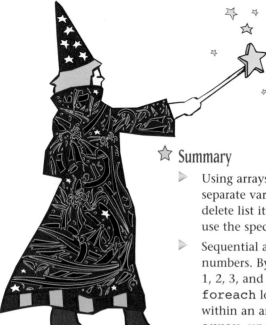

☆ Summary

▷ Using arrays helps you organize data into lists instead of separate variables. Arrays enable your scripts to add and delete list items on a fly, concisely examine list items, and use the special array functions.

▷ Sequential arrays use indices numbered with sequential numbers. By default indices start numbering from 0, then 1, 2, 3, and so on. You can use the `for` loop and `foreach` loop to concisely examine the various items within an array. Functions such as the `array_shift()`, `array_unshift()`, `array_pop()`, `array_push()`, `count()`, `sort()` can be used to manipulate sequential arrays.

▷ Associative arrays use string value indices rather than numerical values. They are useful for cross-referencing an index with a value. You can use the `foreach` loop to concisely examine the various items within an associative array. Functions such as the `array_shift()`, `array_unshift()`, `array_pop()`, `array_push()`, `count()`, `asort()`, and `ksort()` can be used to manipulate associative arrays.

☆ Online References

PHP manual section discussing arrays
`http://www.php.net/manual/en/language.types.array.php`

PHP tutorial with a section covering arrays
`http://hotwired.lycos.com/webmonkey/`

Article describing how to use PHP associative and multidimensional arrays
`http://www.onlamp.com/pub/a/php/2001/06/21/php_foundations.html`

☆ Review Questions

1. What are three advantages of using arrays?

2. What would be the output of the following PHP lines?

```
$pres = array('Washington', 'Adams',
              'Jefferson', 'Madison');
print "$pres[1] and $pres[2] both died on July 4,
              1826.";
```

3. Write a `print` statement that would output the following array in reverse order.

```
$list1 = array('Reading', 'Writing',
'Arithmetic', 'Spelling');
```

4. What two functions can add items to an array? What two functions can delete items from an array? What does each function do?

5. What is the output of the following code?

```
$list1 = array(9, 8, 7, 6, 5);
print "sublist=$list1[2] $list1[4]";
```

6. When might it be advantageous to use an associative array instead of a sequential one?

7. Using the associative array and script lines below, what are the values of $x, $y, and $z?

```
$months = array('Jan'=>31, 'Feb'=>28, 'Mar'=>31,
                'Apr'=>30, 'May'=>31, 'Jun'=>30,
                'Jul'=>31, 'Aug'=>31, 'Sep'=>30,
                'Oct'=>31, 'Nov'=>30, 'Dec'=>31);
$x = $months['Mar'];   $y = $months['Jan'] * 2;
$z = ($months['Mar'] - $months['Feb']);
```

8. What would be the output of the script used for Figure 5.10 if the user selected "Unknown" and entered "Junk" in the calling form shown at the top of Figure 5.10?

9. What are the `unset()` and `isset()` functions used for?

10. What is the difference between each of the following functions: `sort()`, `asort()`, and `ksort()`?

☆ Hands-On Exercises

1. Modify the front-end form and the form-handling script used to create the output in Figure 5.4 to include another question that asks the user to check what he or she likes about the Tuna Café. Create check box items that include the following responses:

   a. The marvelous food preparation
   b. The affordable prices
   c. The speedy service
   d. Just like tuna
   e. None of the above

   Output the user's selections from the form-handling script in a bullet list (like Figure 5.4). Make sure you output a message if the user fails to select anything.

2. Create a front-end form that has eight text boxes that each ask the user to input a number. Add each number to an array and then output the original input data sorted in numerical order. Also output the average, maximum, minimum, and median values. (The median is the value at which half the items are larger and half are smaller.) Don't forget to verify that the user entered something for each text box and that the input values are numbers. (*Hint*: Use the is_numeric() function.) *Optional*: If a text box is left empty, don't include it in the data, but make sure at least one number is entered.

3. Modify the distance calculator script and its front-end form (from Figure 5.8) to enable the user to output all destination cities and distances less than 500 miles, 1000 miles, or 1500 miles. Include a final option to output all cities and distances. Output the destination city and distances sorted by distances.

4. Modify the distance calculator script (and front-end form) from Figure 5.8 to allow the user to determine the distance from Dallas, Texas (or Chicago), to a variety of different destinations. Use the following destination cities and distances from Dallas.

City	Distance to Dallas (in miles)	City	Distance to Dallas (in miles)
Boston	1551	Miami	1108
Chicago	803	Pittsburgh	1069
Nashville	615	San Francisco	1493
Las Vegas	1077	Toronto	1203

Optional: Include a radio button that asks the user if he or she would like all the destination cities and distances output. If selected, output the destination cities and distances sorted alphabetically by destination city.

5. Modify the front-end form and script from Figure 5.12 to enable the user to increment and decrement an inventory count for an item, as well as display part information without changing the inventory count. When the user submits the form, run the selected operation (that is, increment, decrement, or retain the inventory count). Use a foreach loop to output all the indices and items in the array.

6. Create a Web application that provides information about some of the U.S. presidents. Use a front-end form with a check box that allows the user to pick the name of the president about whom the user wants more information. Store the following information in a multidimensional array.

Name	Term	Brief Description
Washington, George	1789–1797	Soldier, statesman, farmer, politician, and commander and chief of the Continental Army during the Revolutionary War.
Adams, John	1797–1801	Farmer, lawyer, political philosopher, diplomat, and politician. He was a leader for U.S. Independence.
Jefferson, Thomas	1801–1809	Architect, scientist, diplomat, author, and politician. He authored the Declaration of Independence.
Madison, James	1809–1817	One of the framers of the Virginia Constitution, the U.S. Bill of Rights, the U.S. Constitution, and the `Federalists Essays`.

Optional: Allow the user to select more than one U.S. president at a time.

Optional: Allow the user to output information about U.S. presidents who served more than four years.

CHAPTER SIX

Matching Patterns and Working with Files

P HP supports a set of pattern-matching functions that use a group of special characters, called *regular expressions*, to enable scripts to search for specific string patterns. Working with patterns in string variables is an important topic since HTML form input appears as character strings to PHP scripts. Using PHP pattern-matching functions with regular expressions enables your PHP scripts to concisely filter undesirable Web input and clarify expected input with the user.

Working with files provides a way for your scripts to store and retrieve data between the times they run. This long-term storage of program data can greatly increase the utility of applications you develop. For example, by using files to store input and output data, a script can look up product inventory data, save a customer order, input initial variable values, increment a page counter, and perform many other tasks.

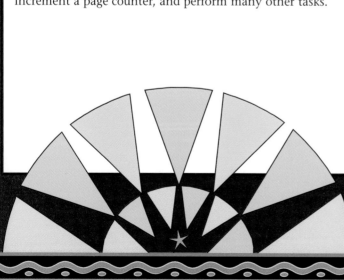

◎◎ Chapter Objectives

☆ To learn to use PHP pattern-matching functions and regular expressions to match character string patterns and filter input data

☆ To learn to work with files to store and retrieve data

◎◎ Working with Patterns in String Variables

The solutions to many programming problems require matching or manipulating patterns in string variables. One reason to match patterns is to verify data received from an HTML input form. For example, if you are expecting an HTML form field to provide a U.S. telephone number as input, your script needs a way to verify that the input comprises a string of seven or ten digits (if including the area code). Another reason to match patterns is if your script uses an input data file with fields delimited by characters such as colons or tabs. For example, say your input file uses a colon as a delimiter, as shown below.

```
FirstName:LastName:Age:Salary
```

Your script needs a way to extract each field from each file input line to process this data (for example, to extract the first name, last name, age, and salary into separate variables).

PHP supports three basic pattern-matching functions called `ereg()`, `split()`, and `ereg_replace()`. These functions all use a special set of pattern-matching characters called **regular expressions** to determine very specific match patterns. Let's concentrate on `ereg()` for now to understand how it works and how you can use it with regular expressions. We will look at `split()` and `ereg_replace()` (briefly) later in this chapter.

Using the ereg() Function

Use the `ereg()` function to determine whether a string contains a particular pattern of characters. It has the basic syntax shown in Figure 6.1.

The function returns *true* if the target string contains the search pattern. Otherwise, the function returns *false*.	Specify the string value or string variable in which to search for the pattern.

```
$ret = ereg("search pattern", "target string");
```

Specify the set of normal or special characters to search for in the target string.

Figure 6.1 General Format of the `ereg()` Function

As you can see in Figure 6.1, the `ereg()` function has two arguments: a **search pattern** and a **target string**. It searches the target string for the search pattern and returns *true* if the search pattern is found and *false* otherwise. For example, consider the following code segment.

```
$name = 'Jake Jackson';
$pattern = 'ke';
if (ereg($pattern, $name)){
   print 'Match';
} else {
   print 'No match';
}
```

The above code outputs "Match" since the string "ke" is found inside the string "Jake Jackson". However, if $pattern was equal to "aa" the above code segment would output "No match" since "aa" does not appear in the string "Jake Jackson".

Using Regular Expressions with the ereg() Function

As previously mentioned, PHP uses a special set of pattern-matching characters called *regular expressions* to determine very specific match patterns. The characters used in regular expressions form a small language, with each special character having a different meaning. The meanings of these regular expression characters are not created arbitrarily in PHP but are defined by an industry standard (that is, the IEEE POSIX 1003.2 standard). Let's now look at how we can use regular expressions to enhance the pattern-matching abilities of the PHP ereg() function.

As an example of using regular expressions, with ereg(), suppose you want to determine whether the pattern "AA" starts a string. Preceding a search pattern with a caret symbol (^) returns a match only when the pattern after the caret symbol starts the target string. Consider the following code segment.

```
$part = 'AA100';
$pattern = '^AA';
if (ereg($pattern, $part)) {
   print 'Match';
} else {
   print 'No match';
}
```

This code segment outputs "Match" since $part starts with "AA". Note, however, this script would output "No match" if $part had value "AB100", "100AA", or "Apple".

Table 6.1 lists several of the regular expression special characters used in PHP and gives an example of each character's use.

Table 6.1 Selected PHP Special Pattern-Matching Characters

Symbol	Meaning
^	*Matches when the following character starts the string.* For example, the following statement is *true* if $name contains "Smith is OK", "Smithsonian", or "Smith, Black". It would be *false* if $name contained only "SMITH" or "Smitty". `if (ereg('^Smith', $name)){`
$	*Matches when the preceding character ends the string.* For example, the statement below would be *true* if $name contains "Joe Johnson", "Jackson", or "This is my son". It would be *false* if $name contained only "My son Jake" or "MY SON". `if (ereg('son$', $name )){`
+	*Matches one or more occurrences of the preceding character.* For example, the statement below is *true* if $name contains "AB101", "ABB101", or "ABBB101 is the right part". It would be *false* if $name contained only "Part A101". `if(ereg('AB+101', $name)){`
*	*Matches zero or more occurrences of the preceding character.* For example, the statement below is *true* if $part starts with "A" and followed by zero or more "B" characters followed by "101", (for example, "AB101", "ABB101", "A101", or "A101 is broke"). It would be *false* if $part contained only "A11". `if (ereg('^AB*101', $part)){`
.	*A wildcard symbol that matches any one character.* For example, the statement is *true* if $name contains "Stop", "Soap", "Szxp", or "Soap is good". It would be *false* if $name contained only "Sxp". `if (ereg('^S..p', $name)){`
|	*An alternation symbol that matches either character pattern.* For example, the statement below would be *true* if $name contains "www.mysite.com", "www.school.edu", "education", or "company". It would be *false* if $name contained only "www.site.net". `if (ereg('com|edu', $name)){`

The following PHP script uses regular expressions with the `ereg()` and `eregi()` functions. The `eregi()` function works like `ereg()` except it uses a case-insensitive comparison. The script provides product information when the user sends a product code to the script. It uses a calling HTML form (with output shown at the top of Figure 6.2) that has the following key HTML form elements.

```
<br>Enter product code (Use AA## format):<br>
      <input type="text" size="6" name="code">
<br> Please enter description:<br>
      <input type="text" size="50" name="description">
```

When the user submits the form, the following script uses `eregi()` to check whether the description contains the words "boat," "Boat", "plane", or "Plane" (since Happy Harry's Hardware doesn't sell boats or planes anymore). Then the script uses `ereg()` to check whether the product code starts with an "AB". If so, the script then checks whether the product code is found, in its associative array of product codes and descriptions and if found it then outputs the product description. The middle of Figure 6.2 shows the output when the user enters *A Big Boat* in the description field. The bottom of the figure shows the output when the user enters product code *AB03* and leaves the description field empty.

```
1.   <html><head><title>Product Information Results </title>
2.   </head><body>
3.   <?php
4.   $products = array('AB01'=>'25-Pound Sledgehammer',
                       'AB02'=>'Extra Strong Nails',
                       'AB03'=>'Super Adjustable Wrench',
                       'AB04'=>'3-Speed Electric Screwdriver');
5.   if (eregi('boat|plane', $description)){
6.       print 'Sorry, we do not sell boats or planes anymore';
7.   } elseif  (ereg('^AB', $code)){
8.       if  (isset($products["$code"])){
9.           print "Code $code Description: $products[$code]";
10.      } else {
11.          print 'Sorry, product code not found';
12.      }
13.  } else {
14.      print 'Sorry, all our product codes start with "AB"';
15.  }
16.  ?> </body></html>
```

Define an associative array of product codes and product descriptions.

Check whether the product code starts with "AB".

Check whether "boat" or "plane" (in upper- or lowercase letters) appears in the description field.

Here's a brief description of the key lines of the script.

☆ Line 4 establishes an associative array with part numbers as indices and part descriptions as values.

☆ Line 5 uses the `eregi()` function to look for "boat" or "plane" with either lower- or uppercase characters in `$description` (input from the calling HTML form).

☆ Line 7 uses `ereg()` to check whether the product code in `$code` (input from the calling form) starts with "AB". If so, line 8 uses `isset()` to check whether the product code has a value in the associative array defined in line 4, and then line 9 outputs the description if found.

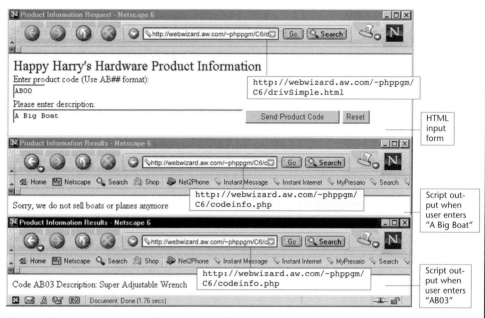

Figure 6.2 HTML Input Form (top) and Sample Outputs (middle, bottom) of a Script That Uses Simple Regular Expressions

Using Grouping Characters

PHP regular expressions use parentheses ((...)), curly brackets ({ ... }), and square brackets ([...]) to specify groups of characters. Each type of grouping character has different meanings. You can combine these groupings with other regular expression special characters to get flexible and specific match patterns. Let's look at each of these grouping characters.

Using Parentheses to Group Characters

Use parentheses to specify a group of characters in a regular expression. For example, the following code line uses parentheses with the alternation character (|) to indicate "Dav" can be followed by "e" or "id".

Match Statement	Possible Matching Values
if (ereg('Dav(e|id)', $name)) {	"Dave", "David", "Dave was here"

You can really see the power of regular expressions when you combine parentheses with other special pattern-matching characters. For example, the following code line uses the alternation operator (|), the caret operator (^), and the dollar sign ($) with parentheses. Note that the string "See David run" would not match.

Match Statement	Possible Matching Values
`if (ereg('^(d|D)av(e|id)$', $name)) {`	"Dave", "David", "dave", "david"

Using Curly Brackets to Specify Character Repetitions

Use curly brackets to specify a range of repetitions of the preceding character. You can specify a specific number, a minimum number, or a range of numbers of repetitions. As shown below, using just a number inside the curly brackets sets a specific number of repetitions. Thus, in the first example below, if $name contained "LLLL" the statement would be *false*. If you include a comma after the number in the curly brackets, you can search for a *minimum* of that many repetitions of the character. (See the second example.) Finally you can match a *minimum* and *maximum* number of repetitions by specifying a range in the curly brackets.

Match Statements	Possible Matching Values
`if (ereg('^L{3}$', $name)){`	"LLL" only
`if (ereg('^L{3,}$', $name)){`	"LLL", "LLLL", "LLLLL", "LLLLLL", and so on
`if (ereg('^L{2,4}$', $name)){`	"LL", "LLL", or "LLLL" only

☆**WARNING** Specifying a Maximum Number of Characters

You can specify a minimum number of repetitions to match without specifying a maximum number. However, you cannot specify a maximum number of repetitions to match unless you also specify a minimum. For example, the line below is *true* if $name has four or more "D" characters.

`if (ereg('^D{4,}$', $name)) {`

However, the following line is *not* valid.

`if (ereg('^D{,4}', $name)) {`

Using Square Brackets to Specify Character Classes

Use square brackets to specify a **character class**. Character classes match *only one* of the characters found between the square brackets. For example, in the line below, the matching pattern must consist of the characters "Sea" followed by "n" or "t" and then followed by an exclamation point. Note that the pattern "Seant!" would not match this pattern.

Match Statement	Possible Matching Values
`if (ereg('Sea[nt]!', $name)){`	"Sean!", "Seat!", "Here comes Sean!"

A more common use of the square brackets is to specify a range of values to match. To specify a range, use a dash (-). For example, [0-9] specifies to match a single number from 0 to 9, [A-Z] specifies a single capital letter from "A" to "Z", and [a-z] specifies a single lowercase letter from "a" to "z". For example, the following pattern matches if a number from 0 to 9 is found in $prodcode.

Match Statement	Possible Matching Values
if (ereg('[0-9]', $prodcode)){	"apple1", "24234", "suzy44", "s1mple"

Because each character class matches only one character, you may need to specify multiple character class operators to search for specific string formats. For example, the following line looks for a pattern of two capital letters followed by a number. It would be *false* if $code contains only "Ab1", "AX", "A111", or "X11".

Match Statement	Possible Matching Values
if (ereg('[A-Z][A-Z][0-9]', $code)){	"AA9", "Send product AZ9", "MY12"

When the caret symbol (^) appears as the first character within the square brackets ([^ . . .]), it means *not*—that is, look for a character *not* matching the pattern in the character class. The following example looks for any character *not* within the range 5–9, then a digit within the range 0–9, then a capital letter. It would not match "51X", "Product 81A", or "AX68A".

Match Statement	Possible Matching Values
if (ereg('[^5-9][0-9][A-Z]', $code)) {	"The AA9A is OK", "Product 44X is down", "It was 9Years ago."

☆ **TIP**   **Different Uses for the Caret Symbol**

The caret symbol (^) has different meanings depending on how it is used. Within a character class, as in [^ . . .], it means *not*. In Table 6.1 you saw how to use it to indicate that the character that follows the caret symbol *starts* the match pattern.

Using Special Character Classes

PHP regular expressions use a set of preset character classes for matching individual items. You can use them for convenience and to add clarity to your regular expressions. For example, to match a single alpha character, you can use [[:alpha:] or you can use ([a-z]|[A-Z]). The two are equivalent, but [[:alpha:]] is a little easier to see and understand. Table 6.2 presents some of PHP's special character classes, their meanings, and examples of their use.

Table 6.2 Selected PHP Special Character Classes

Character Class	Meaning
`[[:space:]]`	*Matches a single space.* For example, the statement below is *true* if `$code` contains the letter "e" followed by a space. So "Apple Core", "Alle y", or "Here you go" matches but not "Alone" or "Fun Time". `if (ereg('e[[:space:]]', $code)) {`
`[[:alpha:]]`	*Matches any word character (uppercase or lowercase letters).* For example, the statement below is *true* if `$code` contains the letter "e" followed by an upper or lower case letter. Therefore, "Times", "Treaty", or "timetogo" matches but not "#%^&", "time", or "Time to go". `if (ereg('e[[:alpha:]]', $code )){`
`[[:upper:]]`	*Matches any single uppercase but not lowercase character.* For example, the code below is *true* if `$code` contains "Home" or "There is our Home" but not "home" or "Our home". `if (ereg('[[:upper:]]ome', $code)){`
`[[:lower:]]`	*Matches any single lowercase but not uppercase character.* For example, the code below is *true* if `$code` contains "home" or "There is our home" but not "Home" or "Our Home". `if (ereg('[[:lower:]]ome', $code)){`
`[[:digit:]]`	*Matches any valid numerical digit (that is, any number 0–9).* For example, the code below is *true* if `$code` contains "B12abc", "The B1 product is late", "I won bingo with a B9", or "Product B00121" but is *false* if `$code` contains "B 0", "Product BX 111", or "Be late 1". `if (ereg('B[[:digit:]]', $code)){`
`[[:punct:]]`	*Matches any punctuation mark.* For example, the statement below is *true* if `$code` contains "AC101!", "Product number.", or "!!" but is *false* if it contains "1212" or "test". `if (ereg('[[:punct:]]$', $code)){`

Building Regular Expressions That Work

As you may have figured out from the previous examples, regular expressions are very powerful—but they can also be virtually unreadable. To build complex regular expressions, start with a simple regular expression and then refine it incrementally. That is, build one piece at a time and test each piece as you go along.

The following example builds a regular expression that looks for a date field in the `mm/dd/yyyy` format (for example, "01/05/2002" but not "1/5/02"). The steps below detail a process for incrementally building a regular expression that would look for input in this format.

1. *Determine the precise field rules.* That is, determine what is valid input and invalid input. For example, if you want to create a text field that accepts only a date field, think through the valid and invalid rules for the field. You might decide to allow "09/09/2002" but neither "9/9/2002" nor "Sep/9/2002" as valid date formats. Work through several examples as listed below.

Rule	Patterns to Reject Given the Rule
1. Accept Only "/" as a separator.	`05 05 2002`, `05-05-2002`
2. Use a four-digit year.	`05/05/02`
3. Accept only date data.	`The date is 05/05/2002`, `05/05/2002 is my date`
4. Require two digits for months and two digits for days.	`5/05/2002`, `05/5/2002`, `5/5/2002`

2. *Get the form and form-handling scripts working.* Build the input form with the form element you want to verify and then build the receiving function or script that accepts the field as input. Make sure these work before you add the regular expressions. For example, a first-pass form-handling script might contain the script lines below. Notice that the regular expression requires that at least one character be input for `$date`; no other validation is performed.

```
if (ereg('.+', $date)){
   print "Valid date= $date";
} else {
   print "Invalid date= $date";
}
```

> `$date` must contain one or more characters

3. *Start with the most specific term possible.* For example, slashes must separate the two characters (for the month), followed by two more characters (for the day), followed by four characters (for the year). Therefore, you can change the first line above to the following:

```
if (ereg('../../....', $date )){
```

This code requires exactly two characters, then "/", then two more characters, then "/", then four characters. Thus in the above regular expression, "12/21/1234" and "fj/12/ffff" are valid, but "1/1/11" is not.

4. *Anchor the parts you can.* Add the ^ and $ quantifiers where possible. Also, add the `[[:digit:]]` character class to require numbers instead of just any character.

```
$two='[[:digit:]]{2}';
if (ereg("^$two/$two/$two$two$", $date)) {
```

Match exactly two digits.

Now we are getting close to a useful regular expression because "01/16/2003", "09/09/2005", "01/12/1211", and "99/99/9999" are recognized as valid dates.

5. *Get more specific if possible.* After examining the output, you might add the following rules.

   a. The first digit of the month can be only 0 or 1. For example, "25/12/2002" is an illegal date.

   b. The first digit of a day can be only 0, 1, 2, or 3. For example, "05/55/2002" is an illegal date.

   c. Only use years from this century, so filter out dates like "05/05/1928" and "05/05/3003".

The code below follows these rules by specifying [0-3] in the first digit of the days field and [0-1] in the first digit of the months field and by requiring that the first digit of the year field start with 2.

```
$two='[[:digit:]]{2}';
$month='[0-1][[:digit:]]';
$day='[0-3][[:digit:]]';
$year="2[[:digit:]]$two";
if (ereg("^($month)/($day)/($year)$", $date)) {
```

Specify "0" or "1" followed by a number for the month.

Specify "0", "1", "2", or "3" followed by a number for the day.

Specify "2" followed by three numbers for the year.

Now the regular expression recognizes input like "09/99/2001" and "05/05/4000" as illegal.

The following sample PHP script uses the regular expression we just developed to validate a date input from an HTML form. The top of Figure 6.3 shows the form used to request a date and start this script. It uses the following HTML text box input form element.

```
<input type="text" size="10" maxlength="10" name="date">
```

The middle screen of Figure 6.3 shows the response when the user enters an invalid date. The bottom screen shows the response when the user enters a valid date.

```
1.   <html>
2.   <head><title>Date Check</title></head>
3.   <body>
4.   <?php
5.       $two='[[:digit:]]{2}';
6.       $month='[0-1][[:digit:]]';
7.       $day='[0-3][[:digit:]]';
8.       $year="2[[:digit:]]$two";
9.       if (ereg("^($month)/($day)/($year)$", $date)){
10.          print "Valid date=$date <br>";
```

Use the regular expression developed in the previous example to check the date format.

```
11.     } else {
12.         print "Invalid date=$date";
13. }
14. ?></body></html>
```

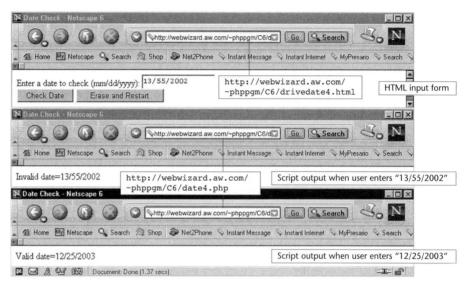

Figure 6.3 HTML Input Form (top) and Sample Outputs (middle, bottom) of a Script That Uses a Regular Expression to Validate a Date Field

☆ **WARNING** Validity Checks for Dates

The code in the script shown here still accepts dates such as 02/30/2002 as valid. Additional validity checking is required to prevent acceptance of such dates from the input form. We will do a little more checking in the example script associated with Figure 6.5.

Matching Patterns with the split() Function

Until now, we have mainly been using the `ereg()` function with regular expressions. The `split()` function is another function that uses regular expressions. Use `split()` to break a string into different pieces based on the presence of a match pattern. It has the general syntax shown in Figure 6.4.

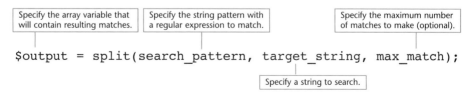

Figure 6.4 General Format of the `split()` Function

The `split()` function breaks the target string into pieces and leaves the results in the output array variable. The target string splits into as many pieces as there are matches for the search pattern unless a maximum number of matches is set in the `max_match` argument. To see how the `split()` function works, examine the following script lines.

```
$line = 'Please , pass        thepepper';
$result = split('[[:space:]]+', $line);
```

Match one or more spaces.

These lines set the `$result` array to each character group separated by one or more spaces. Thus the `$result` array will contain the following values.

```
$result[0] = 'Please';
$result[1] = ','
$result[2] = 'pass';
$result[3] = 'thepepper';
```

As another example, the following code breaks `$line` into pieces using a comma (`,`) as a delimiter.

```
$line = 'Baseball, hot dogs, apple pie';
$item =  split(',', $line);
print ("0=$item[0] 1=$item[1] 2=$item[2]");
```

These lines output "0=Baseball 1= hot dogs 2= apple pie".

When you know how many matches to expect, it is sometimes useful to provide a list of variables that will receive the split fields instead of an array variable name. The following example uses the `list()` function to assign a list of variables as the result of the `split()` function.

```
$line = 'AA1234:Hammer:122:12';
list($partno, $part, $num, $cost) = split(':', $line, 4);
print "partno=$partno part=$part num=$num cost=$cost";
```

The above code outputs "partno=AA1234 part=Hammer num=122 cost=12".

☆ **TIP**   Using `split()` with Files

This example shows how to use `split()` to access information from a string variable with a colon delimiter. The `split()` function is often used this way when data are stored in files. Working with files is covered later in this chapter.

The following script further refines the date validation script associated with Figure 6.3 and uses regular expressions and the `split()` function. It illustrates that some checking of fields may still be needed even after using regular expressions. For example, line 10 in the script uses `split()` to break the `$date` field into `$mon`, `$day`, and `$year`. With these fields split, the script can more completely check these fields for validity than is possible with regular expressions alone (for example, it can check whether $month is between 1 and 12). The top screen of Figure 6.5 shows the form that starts the script and uses the following key HTML form element.

```
<input type="text" size="10" maxlength="10" name="date">
```

The middle screen of Figure 6.5 shows the output when the user enters invalid input, and the bottom screen shows the output when the user enters a valid date.

```
1.  <html><head><title>Date Check</title></head>
2.  <body>
3.  <?php
4.      $two='[[:digit:]]{2}';
5.      $month='[0-1][[:digit:]]';
6.      $day='[0-3][[:digit:]]';
7.      $year="2[[:digit:]]$two";
8.      if (ereg("^($month)/($day)/($year)$", $date)) {
9.          list($mon, $day, $year) = split('/', $date);
10.         if ($mon >= 1 && $mon <= 12){
11.             if ($day <= 31) {
12.                 print "Valid date mon=$mon day=$day year=$year";
13.             } else {
14.                 print " Illegal day specified Day=$day";
15.             }
16.         } else {
17.             print " Illegal month specified Mon=$mon";
18.         }
19.     } else {
20.     print ("Invalid date format= $date");
21.     ?></body></html>
```

> Use the same regular expression used in the script for Figure 6.3.

> Split the month, day, and year from the input variable $date.

Here's a summary of this script.

☆ Lines 4–8 use the same regular expression to check dates as does the script from Figure 6.3.

☆ Line 9 uses the split() function to split the $date variable using slashes (/) as delimiters. It splits the $date string variable into $mon, $day, and $year using the list() function.

☆ Line 10 checks for valid $mon (month) input that is a number from 1 to 12.

☆ Line 11 checks that $day (day) is not greater than 31.

☆ Line 12 outputs an appropriate message if all the input is valid.

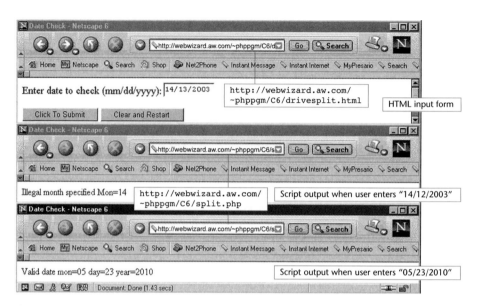

Figure 6.5 HTML Input Form (top) and Sample Outputs (middle, bottom) of a Script That Uses the `split()` Function

☆ SHORTCUT **Use `ereg_replace()` When Replacing Characters in a String Variable**

PHP supports an additional function, called `ereg_replace()`, that uses regular expressions. You can use it to replace one string pattern for another in a string variable. Consider the following code segment.

```
$start = 'AC1001:Hammer:15:150';
$end = ereg_replace('Hammer', 'Drill', $start);
print "end=$end";
```

The above script segment outputs "end=AC1001:Drill:15:150".

◉◉ Working with Files from PHP Scripts

Although the scripts we have created so far can accept input data from the user, they cannot store data values between sessions of running the script. For example, the multidimensional inventory example in Chapter Five (Figure 5.12) uses the same initial values for the inventory each time the script is started. If an inventory count changes or items are deleted, then the script code needs to change. This section describes how to work with files in your PHP scripts. If you are using a UNIX operating system, you may wish to review Appendix B, which discusses setting UNIX file permissions and where to store UNIX data files.

Reading a File into an Array

The easiest way to read a file from a PHP script is to use the `file()` function to read the entire file into an array. The `file()` function takes the name of the file as a single argument and returns an array with each array item set as a line from the file. For example, the following code uses `file()` to read a file called `mydata.txt` (which resides in the same directory as the script) into the `$infile` array. It then outputs the first and third lines of the file.

```
$inf ='mydata.txt';
$infile = file ($inf);
print "$infile[0]";        Output the first line of the file.
print "$infile[2]";        Output the third line of the file.
```

If the file `mydata.txt` contained

```
Apples are red.
Bananas are yellow.
Carrots are orange.
Dates are brown.
```

then the output of the above script would be

```
Apples are red.
Carrots are orange.
```

Although the above script works perfectly well with small input files, reading a very large file into an array is not very efficient (it consumes a lot of memory). So let's look at ways to open files and read them more efficiently. We will also describe how to write to files.

Opening Files

You can use the `fopen()` function to connect a PHP script to a physical data file on a Web server. Once this connection is made, your script will then be able to work with the file. For example, the code shown in Figure 6.6 opens the file stored at `/home/phppgm/data/data.txt` for read-only access (that is, your script will be able to read the file but not write to it).

```
$fileloc = '/home/phppgm/data/data.txt';
$file_ptr = fopen ($fileloc, 'r');
```

Use this file handle in your program to refer to the file.	Specify the filename of the file that exists on the Web server.	Specify file open mode. (`r` means read-only access.)

Figure 6.6 General Format of the `fopen()` Function

As you can see in Figure 6.6, the `fopen()` function returns a **file handle**, which is a variable name you use to refer to the file once your script connects to it. If the `fopen()` function fails it will return *false*. The `fopen()` function uses the following two main arguments:

1. The **filename** defines the name of the file that your script will open. If the file resides in the same file system directory as your script, then you need to specify only the filename (and not the entire file path).

2. The **file open mode** defines the way your script will use the file. The different file open modes include *read-only*, *write-only*, and *append*, among others. Table 6.3 defines the various file open modes.

Table 6.3 File Open Modes for Use with the `fopen()` Function

Open Mode	Description
r	**Read-only mode** opens the file for reading but not writing.
r+	**Read and write mode** opens the file for reading and writing.
w	**Write-only mode** opens a file for writing. If the file exists, it over-writes the existing file when writing. If the file doesn't exist, it creates a new file.
w+	**Read and write overwrite mode** opens the file for writing and reading. If the file exists, it overwrites the existing file when writing. If the file doesn't exist, it creates a new file.
a	**Append mode** opens the file for writing but will append any data written to the end of the existing file. If the file doesn't exist, this command creates a new file.
a+	**Read and append mode** opens the file for writing and reading. Any written data is appended to the existing file. If the file doesn't exist, writing data will create a new file.

As stated above, the `fopen()` function normally returns a file handle to your script. However, if the function fails, it will return *false*. Reasons for failure include improper file access permissions (see Appendix B about UNIX files) and incorrect specification of the file's directory location. If the `fopen()` function fails you likely do not want your script to continue since any further processing would likely be wrong. So, it is good practice to test for an `fopen()` failure and, if it occurs, to end the script. For example, consider the following script.

```
$inf = '/home/phppgm/data/mydata.txt';
$FILEH = fopen($inf, 'r') or die ("Cannot open $inf");
```
Run die() only if fopen() fails.

The second PHP line above attempts to open the file `/home/phppgm/data/mydata.txt`. If it fails, the `die()` function will output the message enclosed in quotes and then terminate the script. Note that the `or` operator is similar to the `||` logical test operator except, unlike `||`, the `or` operator will not run the `die()` function unless `fopen()` fails.

Once you open a file, you can use the `fgets()` function to read from the file one line at a time. The `fgets()` function has the general format shown in Figure 6.7.

This variable receives the characters read from the file.	Specify the file handle of the file used in the `fopen()` function.	This optional argument indicates one or more than the maximum number of bytes to read.

```
$var = fgets(filehandle, length);
```

Figure 6.7 General Format of the `fgets()` Function

As you can see in Figure 6.7, `fgets()` reads a line from the file that the file handle refers to and sets `$var` to contain the characters of that line. The script will read until the end of the line or until the limit set by the length argument is reached. (The length argument became optional starting in PHP version 4.2.0.)

Let's look at an example that uses a `while` loop and the `fopen()` and `fgets()` functions to read each line from `mydata.txt` one line at a time. The script below also uses the `feof()` function to test whether the file pointer is currently at the end-of-file. The function returns *false* when the file is at the end-of-file and *true* otherwise.

```
1. $inf ='mydata.txt';
2. $FILEH = fopen($inf, 'r') or die ("Cannot open $inf");
3. $inline = fgets($FILEH, 4096);        Read the first line of the file.
4. while (!feof($FILEH)) {               Loop until the end of the file is reached.
5.     print "$inline";
6.     $inline = fgets($FILEH, 4096);    Read the next line of the file.
7. }
8. fclose ($FILEH);
```

In this script, line 2 opens the file `mydata.txt`, and then line 3 reads the first line. Lines 4–7 first test to determine whether the file pointer is at the end of the file, then output the line just read and get the next line. When the end of the file is hit, line 8 closes the connection to the file. So, let's assume that the file `mydata.txt` contains the same four lines as before.

```
Apples are red.
Bananas are yellow.
Carrots are orange.
Dates are brown.
```

Then the above script will output each of those lines.

Now let's look at a complete example of reading a file into a script. This example uses an input file called `infile.txt` that contains the following four lines:

```
AC1000:Hammers:122:12.50
AC1001:Wrenches:5:5.00
AC1002:Handsaws:10:10.00
AC1003:Screwdrivers:222:3.00
```

This application revisits the inventory information application from Chapter Five (Figure 5.12), which invites the user to input a product ID and provides information about that product. It uses a front-end form that asks the user to select a product ID (see the top of Figure 6.8) with the following key HTML form element:

```
<input type="radio" name="id" value=$item>
```

When the user submits the form, the application opens the `infile.txt` file and reads the data one line at a time while searching for the input product ID in `$id`. When the product ID is found, the script below outputs the product information in an HTML table. The bottom of Figure 6.8 shows the output of the script when the user submits "AC1002" as the product ID.

```
1.  <html><head><title>Hardware Inventory</title></head><body>
2.  <font size="5" color="blue"> Happy Harry's Hardware Inventory
3.  <br></font><?php
4.      $inf='/home/phppgm/data/infile.txt';
5.      $FILEH = fopen($inf, 'r') or die ("Cannot open $inf");
6.      $inline = fgets($FILEH, 4096);
7.      $found=0;
8.      while (!feof($FILEH) && !($found)) {
9.          list($ptno,$ptname,$num,$price) = split (':',$inline);
10.         if ($ptno == $id) {
11.             print '<table border=1>';
12.             print '<th> ID <th> Part <th> Count <th> Price ';
13.             print "<tr><td> $ptno </td><td>$ptname</td>";
14.             print "<td> $num </td><td>\$$price</td></tr>";
15.             print '</table>';
16.             $found = 1;
17.         }
18.         $inline = fgets($FILEH, 4096);
19.     }
20.     if ($found != 1) {
21.         print "Error: PartNo=$id not found";
22.     }
23.     fclose ($FILEH);
24. ?></body></html>
```

Callouts:
- Line 8: Repeat until the end of the file or until $found does not have value 0.
- Line 10: Check whether the part number from the file ($ptno) matches $id.
- Line 16: Set the value of $found to 1 if $ptno matches $id.
- Line 18: Read the next input line of the file.

Let's briefly review the key lines of the script.

☆ Line 5 uses the `fopen()` function to connect to the file `/home/phppgm/data/infile.txt` and specifies read-only access.

☆ Lines 6 uses the `fgets()` function to read the first line of the file and puts the result into the variable `$inline`.

☆ Line 7 sets `$found` equal to 0. This variable will be set to 1 if a valid part number for `$id` is found in the input file.

☆ Line 8 starts a `while` loop that repeats until the end of the file or until the part number is found (that is, until `$found` equals 1).

☆ Line 9 uses the `split()` function to break the input line into pieces using a colon as the field separator. This function copies the fields in the order in which they are encountered into the variables `$ptno`, `$ptname`, `$num`, and `$price`.

☆ Lines 10–17 first check whether `$ptno` matches the value of `$id` received from the user. If so, the script creates an HTML table and outputs the values of `$ptno`, `$ptname`, `$num`, and `$price`. Line 16 also sets `$found` equal to 1 to end the `while` loop on its next iteration.

☆ Line 20 checks whether `$found` does not have a value of 1. If so, then the input `$id` value was not found during the `while` loop and an error message is output.

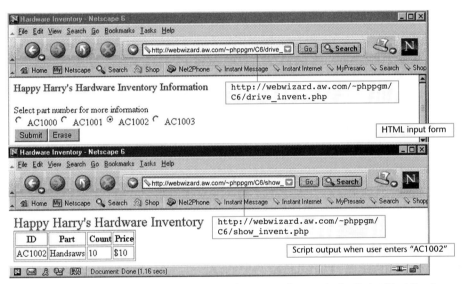

Figure 6.8 HTML Input Form (top) and Sample Output (bottom) of a Script That Reads and Outputs a File

Writing to Files

Writing to files is a useful way to store data between times your program runs. Once you successfully open a file for writing, you can write to your file by using the `fputs()` function. The `fputs()` function accepts two arguments: a file handle and text to output. Figure 6.9 shows the general format of the `fputs()` function.

```
$message = "My script was here";
$ret = fputs($OFILE, $message);
```

The function returns the number of bytes written to the file or *false* (if an error ocurrs).

Specify the file handle of the file to access for writing.

Specify the data to output to the file.

Figure 6.9 General Format of the `fputs()` Function

The PHP code segment in Figure 6.9 writes the line "My script was here" to the file referenced by the file handle $OFILE. As another example, here is a script segment that opens a file and writes the line "Apples are red" to it.

```
$inf ='/home/phppgm/data/log.txt';
$FILEH = fopen($inf, 'w') or die("Cannot open $inf");
fputs($FILEH, 'Apples are red');
fclose ($FILEH);
```

Recall that since the above script segment opens the file in write-only mode, if the file exists before this script segment is carried out, the output of the script will overwrite the file contents. Also note that if you're using a UNIX Web server, the file must be set with write permission for anyone. (See Appendix B.)

Example: Appending Data

Recall that if you open a file in a or a+ mode that you can append data to a file. A good application for appending data to files involves logging information to files. The next script opens a file and appends user comments to the end of it. The script uses the date() function to get the current month, day, and time and then appends the user comments received from the calling form to the comments.txt file. The HTML form uses the following key HTML form element.

```
<br><textarea rows="1" cols="50" name="comments"></textarea>
```

The top screen shot in Figure 6.10 shows the form that sends comments to the script. The bottom screen shot shows the output of the following PHP script.

```
1.  <html> <head><title>Log Comments</title></head><body>
2.  <?php
3.     $logfile='/home/phppgm/data/comments.txt';
4.     $OUTF = fopen($logfile, 'a+') or die("Cannot open
          $logfile");
5.     $today = date('m/d/Y:h:m');
6.     $msg = "$today:$comments\n";
7.     print "Just Logged: <br> $msg";
8.     fputs($OUTF, $msg);
9.     fclose($OUTF);
10. ?>
11. </body></html>
```

Here's a brief summary of this script.

☆ Lines 3–4 identify the location of the log file (/home/phppgm/data/comments.txt) and then open this file in read and append mode.

☆ Line 5 uses the date() function to get the current month, day, year, hour, and minute.

☆ Line 6 sets the $msg variable to include the date information and the contents of $comments (from the calling form).

☆ Lines 7–8 output the contents of $msg to the browser and then to the log file. Line 9 closes the log file.

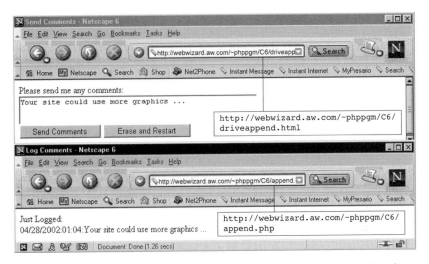

Figure 6.10 HTML Input Form (top) and Output (bottom) of the Comment-Logging Script

---

☆ **SHORTCUT Use a Consistent Field Separator**

This example uses a colon to separate the date and comments fields. Using a field separator such as a colon or tab character makes it easier to read and interpret the data later because you can read one line at a time and use `split()` to get each input field.

☆ **WARNING These Examples Are Just That—Examples**

Carefully consider security issues before writing any script that allows users to write to files across the Internet. For example, the script for Figure 6.10 needs some measures to ensure that the log file does not get too large, for example, because of a hacker consuming all the disk space on the server by logging comment after comment. Making an application secure is your responsibility as a developer. For more information on security, review the World Wide Web Consortium's security FAQs at `http://www.w3.org/Security/Faq/www-security-faq.html`.

Locking a File Before Writing

Web applications have the potential to allow many users to run the same script simultaneously. For example, two or more users might access an inventory update script concurrently. If multiple users access scripts that attempt to write to the same file at the same time, they could corrupt the file. A corrupted file is usually an unintelligible mixture of data that is useless to your script.

PHP provides the `flock()` function to ensure that only one PHP script at a time can write data to a file. It has the general format shown in Figure 6.11.

Specify the lock type. LOCK_EX means only one
program at a time can read/write to the file.

```
$ret = flock($FHILE, LOCK_EX);
```

If an error occurs, the function
returns a value of *false*.

Specify the file handle
of the file to lock.

Figure 6.11 General Format of the `flock()` Function

As you can see in Figure 6.11, the `flock()` function accepts two arguments: *a file handle* and a *lock type*. For our purposes we use a lock type of LOCK_EX, which requests an *exclusive* lock and ensures only one script at a time can read and write to the file. As an example, the following code opens a file handle in write-only-append mode, uses `flock()` to get exclusive access to the file, and writes a line to the end of the file.

```
$outf='/home/phppgm/data/mydata2.txt';
$OUTF = fopen($outf, 'a') or die ("Cannot open $outf");
flock($OUTF, LOCK_EX) or die ("Cannot lock file $outf");
fputs($OUTF, 'My script was here\n') or die("Write error
$outf");
fclose($OUTF);
```

These PHP lines append "My script was here" to the file `mydata2.txt` stored at `/home/phppgm/data/mydata2.txt`.

☆ **TIP**   **Remember the New Line Character**

Use the \n character to output a new line character into the file. If you omit the new line character, the appended text will appear together on the same line if you run the script twice, for example:

```
My script was hereMy script was here
```

Because the script used in the example in this section does use a new line character, your file will contain the following if you run that script twice:

```
My script was here
My script was here
```

Reading and Writing Files

The solutions to some programming problems require a script to read and write data while the script runs. The most straightforward way to read and write from the same file is to use the `rewind()` function, which has the following general format:

If an error occurs, the function returns a value of *false.*

```
$ret = rewind(filehandle);
```

Specify the file handle of a previously opened file.

Figure 6.12 General Format of the `rewind()` Function

The `rewind()` function resets the file position indicator back to the start of the file. For example, the following sequence of code opens a file, reads the first line, resets the file pointer to the start of the file, and then overwrites the first character in that file with the letter "Z".

```
1. $FILEH = fopen('myfile.txt', 'r+');        Read the first line.
2. $inline = fgets($FILEH, 4096);
3. rewind($FILEH);                             Reset the file pointer
                                               to the start of the file.
4. $ret= fputs($FILEH, 'Z');
                                               Overwrite the first character
                                               of the first line.
```

Let's say the file `myfile.txt` contains the following lines.

```
A
B
C
```

After we run this script segment, the file will contain the following lines.

```
Z
B
C
```

☆**WARNING** The `rewind()` Function Does Not Work for Append Mode

If you open a file in append mode (a or a+) the `rewind()` function will not work. Any writes you perform will continue to append data to the end of the file despite the use of `rewind()` in your script.

The next script implements a simple Web page hit counter using the `flock()` and `rewind()` functions. This example opens a counter file at `/home/phppgm/logfiles/ctr.txt` for reading and writing, locks the file, and then reads and increments its counter value. Next, the script rewinds the counter file, writes the new page count value, and closes the file. Note that line 6 uses the `rtrim()` function to remove a new line character (\n) if it exists at the end of the input line.

```
1.  <?php
2.  $ctfile='/home/phppgm/logfiles/ctr.txt';
3.  $FILEH = fopen($ctfile, 'r+') or die ("Cannot open $ctfile");
4.  flock($FILEH, LOCK_EX) or die ("Cannot lock file $outf");
5.  $ctr = fgets($FILEH, 4096) or die ("Cannot gets $ctfile");
6.  $ctr = rtrim($ctr, '\n');        Remove \n if it exists in the file's input line.
```

Working with Files from PHP Scripts

```
7.    if (is_numeric($ctr)){
8.        $count= $ctr + 1;
9.        rewind ($FILEH);
10.       $ret= fputs($FILEH, $count);
11.       print ("$count");
12.    } else {
13.       print "Error: ctr=$ctr <=not numeric value";
14.    }
15.    fclose ($FILEH);
16.    ?>
```

Make sure the file input data is numeric.

Reset the file pointer to the start of the file and save the new count value.

Let's review the script's key lines.

☆ Lines 2–3 set the location of the counter file and open it for reading and writing.

☆ Line 4 locks the file with an exclusive lock.

☆ Lines 5 reads the contents of the counter file, and then line 6 trims off a new line character (\n) if it exists at the end of the file's input line. (Sometimes this character is inadvertently present in files created on a UNIX Web server.)

☆ Line 7 makes sure the input data is a numeric value. A non-numeric value is not expected but might occur if the file is corrupted.

☆ Lines 8–9 add 1 to the file access count (in $ctr) and then rewind the file to set the file pointer back to the start of the file.

☆ Lines 10–11 first write the new value of the counter variable to the file and then output that value to the browser.

One way to use the above counter script is to store it in a file and then include it within an HTML document. Use the following line in your HTML document to call the previous script if it's stored in counter.php.

```
<?php include 'counter.php' ?>
```

As an example, consider the following short HTML document that calls the counter.php script. The output of the script is shown in Figure 6.12.

```
<html><head><title>Harry's Place </title>
</head><body>
<font size="5" color="blue">Happy Harry's Hardware Home</font>
<br>Hit Count:<?php include 'counter.php' ?>
</body></html>
```

☆ **TIP   A Variation on Counters**

One fanciful way to display page count values is to create (or obtain from the Internet) graphic files that represent each digit you want to display and then to use those graphic files to output the current page count. For example, you may have files called one.gif, two.gif, three.gif, and so on. If you want to display the number 35, for example, you could display three.gif and five.gif next to each other.

Figure 6.13 Output of an HTML Document Using the Page Counter Script

Another File Read/Write Example: Creating an Online Survey

The next script is a little more extensive example of reading and writing with files. This application creates a survey focused on favorite tools at Happy Harry's Hardware. This survey script is called from a form shown at the top of Figure 6.14. This calling form uses the following key HTML form elements.

```
<input type="radio" name="tool" value="hammer" checked> Hammer
<input type="radio" name="tool" value="wrench"> Wrench
<input type="radio" name="tool" value="sdriver"> Screwdriver
<input type="radio" name="tool" value="fryingpan"> Frying Pan
```

The bottom portion of Figure 6.14 shows the output of the survey script, which stores the survey results into the file /home/phppgm/data/survey1.txt. If you're using a UNIX Web server, the survey file needs to be created with read and write permissions for anyone. (See Appendix B.) The file holds the current vote total for each survey option (hammer, wrench, screwdriver, and frying pan) separated by colons. For example, the initial contents of this file would be:

```
0:0:0:0
```

The survey script appears below.

```
1.  <html><head><title>Happy Harry's Hardware Survey </title>
2.  </head><body>
3.  <font size="5" color="blue">Survey Results</font>
4.  <?php
5.  $ctfile='/home/phppgm/data/survey1.txt';
6.  $SURVEY = fopen($ctfile, 'r+') or die("Cannot open $ctfile");
7.  flock($SURVEY, LOCK_EX) or die ("Cannot lock file $ctfile");
8.  $inline = fgets($SURVEY, 4096);
9.  list($hammer, $wrench, $sdriver, $fpan) = split(':', $inline);
10. if ($tool == 'hammer'){
11.     $hammer = $hammer + 1;
12. } elseif ($tool == 'sdriver') {
13.     $sdriver = $sdriver + 1;
14. } elseif ($tool == 'wrench'){
15.     $wrench = $wrench + 1;
16. } elseif ($tool == 'fryingpan'){
17.     $fpan = $fpan + 1;
```

Line 8–9 note: Split the line input from file using ":" as separator

Lines 10–17 note: Increment the vote total for the matching tool

```
18. } else {
19.   die ('ERROR: Illegal call');
20. }
```
> Calculate total number of votes received.
```
21. $ct=$hammer + $sdriver + $wrench + $fpan;
22. print "<br>Hammer=$hammer Wrench=$wrench
            Screwdriver=$sdriver Frying Pan=$fpan Total votes=$ct";
23. rewind($SURVEY);
```
> Save the new vote totals.
```
24. $ret= fputs($SURVEY, "$hammer:$wrench:$sdriver:$fpan");
25. fclose ($SURVEY);
26. ?></body></html>
```

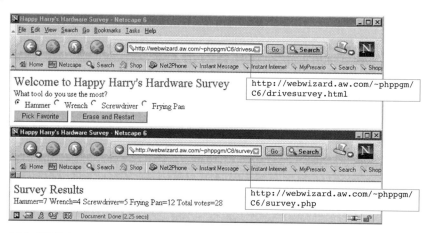

Figure 6.14 HTML Input Form (top) and Sample Output (bottom) from the Survey Script

Here's a summary of the key lines of the script.

☆ Lines 5–6 set the location of the survey file and then open the file.

☆ Line 7 locks the file with an exclusive lock.

☆ Lines 8–9 read the first (and only) line from the input file into the `$inline` array and then uses the `split()` and `list()` functions to split the `$inline` array using a colon as a field separator.

☆ Lines 10–20 use the value of `$tool` (received from the calling form) to decide which tool the user picked. That tool's vote total is then incremented by 1. Line 19 outputs an error message if `$tool` does not match a valid tool type.

☆ Lines 21–22 calculate the total votes received and then output the new survey totals.

☆ Lines 23–24 use the `rewind()` function to reset the file pointer and then write the new results to the survey file.

☆ **TIP**   **Additional File Functions**

PHP supports several other file functions you can use to do things like check whether a file exists, check the size of a file, and determine the last time the file was modified (among many other things). See `http://www.php.net/filesystem` for more details.

☆ Summary

▷ PHP supports a set of three functions [that is, `ereg()`, `split()`, and `ereg_replace()`] that are useful for matching and manipulating patterns in strings. These functions use regular expressions to greatly enhance their pattern-matching capabilities. Regular expressions enable a script to look for specific characters (such as numbers, words, or letters) in specific places in a string.

▷ Working with files enables a script to store data for long periods of time. You can use data files to input data into scripts and to store script results. Use the `fgets()` function to read lines from a file into a program. Use the `fputs()` function to write lines to a file. Both functions require that you first open the file with the `fopen()` function using the proper open mode.

☆ Online References

PHP online manual section discussing files and file I/O
`http://www.php.net/filesystem`

PHP tutorial covering file I/O
`http://www.technobreeze.net/php/tutorial/tutorial.files.html`

PHP tutorial covering regular expressions
`http://www.webreference.com/programming/php/regexps/`

Online PHP tutorial that includes sections on regular expressions and file I/O
`http://jamhitz.tripod.com/`

☆ Review Questions

1. Write a statement that checks whether the value of `$name` contains the sequence "ABC". Write another statement that checks whether the value of `$name` contains either "ABC" or "DEF".

2. What output would the script used for Figure 6.2 give for each of the following input values for `$code` and `$description`?

   a. `$code = 'AbV109'; $descpription = 'Small hammer';`
   b. `$code = 'AB1'; $description = 'A wood planer';`
   c. `$code = 'AC1009'; $description = 'Adjustable spanner';`

3. Show two possible values for $name that would make the following test condition *true*. Show one possible value for $name that would result in it being *false*.

```
$one='[[:digit:]]';
if (ereg("^..$one$one", $name)){
```

4. What is each of the following character classes used for? `[[:space:]]`, `[[:alpha:]]`, `[[:upper:]]`, `[[:lower:]]`, `[[:digit:]]`, and `[[:punct:]]`.

5. What are each of the following PHP special pattern-matching characters used for? `^`, `$`, `+`, `*`, `.`, and `|`.

6. Suppose you want the script used for Figure 6.3 to accept as input only dates in October. How would you change lines 5–9 of this script (shown below)?

```
$two='[[:digit:]]{2}';
$month='[0-1][[:digit:]]';
$day='[0-3][[:digit:]]';
$year="2[[:digit:]]$two";
if (ereg("^($month)/($day)/($year)$", $date)){
```

7. What is the output of the following code?

```
$line = 'XYZ123:12.50:22:Big and Green';
$parsed = split(':', $line);
print "$parsed[1] $parsed[2]";
```

8. What is a file handle? What is it used for?

9. What are the six different file open modes?

10. Why is it necessary to lock a file? What function do you use to lock it?

11. What does the `rewind()` function do?

☆ Hands-On Exercises

1. Create a front-end form that asks the user to enter a seven-digit phone number. Use a PHP script (with regular expressions) to verify that the input has one of the following formats.

   a. Allow only seven digits. Do not allow dashes or other characters to be specified.

   b. Allow an optional dash between the third and fourth digits—that is, `345-1234`.

   c. Allow an optional dash or space between the third and fourth digits—that is, `345 1234`, `3451234`, or `345-1234`.

2. Create a form that asks the user to create a user ID and password. The user ID and password must conform to a set of rules to be valid (see below). Generate an appropriate message to output upon receiving an invalid user ID or password. Use the following rules for these input fields.

    a. User IDs must start with a character (a–z) and be at least three characters long. Capital letters are not allowed anywhere in the user ID (for example, as in `hotDog` or `myLogin`). User IDs also cannot include spaces, dashes, or any other special characters (such as "!", "@", "#", "$", or "%"). Finally, user IDs cannot be one of the "reserved" user IDs, which include `root`, `admin`, and `operator`.

    b. The password field must be at least six characters long. Passwords must be valid letters or numbers and cannot include spaces, dashes, or any other special characters (such as "!", "@", "#", and "$").

    Optional: Extend the script so that when a valid user ID and password is received, it checks a file on your server to see whether the user ID exists. If it does exist, inform the user to select another user ID. If it doesn't already exist, append the password and user ID to the end of the file and notify the user that he or she successfully created a new user ID and password.

3. Create a script that reads a file and produces a Web-based report for each "product" in the file. The file will be a set of four fields, each separated from the next by a colon, with the following format:

    `Partnumber:Number Sold:Price:Number Available:Cost`

    For each line in the file, the report should indicate:

    ✯ The part number

    ✯ The total revenue it generated—that is, `Price * Number Sold`

    ✯ The total cost of the inventory remaining—that is, `Number Available * Cost`

    For example, with the input

    `AX1001:2:10:20:5`

    the output would be

    `Part Number: AX1001 Total Revenue: 20 Inventory Cost: 100`

    You can find a sample file at `http://webwizard.aw.com/~phppgm/C6/6.3.Input.txt` Make sure you use regular expressions to validate each input field received.

4. Write an application that stores journal entries in a file. Use a front-end form that asks for a password (use `pass123` as a password) and has a text box that asks for a journal entry. When the user submits the form, save the date

and journal entry appended to a file on the Web server. Use a field separator such as a tab character or colon between the date and journal entry. *Optional*: Provide another form that asks the user to enter a date and a password (use `pass123` again) and then displays the journal entry for that day. Make sure the date is in the correct format.

5. Write an application that creates a Web survey that asks the user to "vote" for one of four choices. When the user votes, output the current vote totals and the percentage of the overall total for each choice. (Make sure that the application can handle any illegal input). *Optional*: Provide a super-secret input sequence that resets the survey results in the file. This input sequence would not appear on the user's form but could be set only by specifying it from a special form or by entering it from a URL using `password=reset00`.

6. Modify the file counter example from Figure 6.13 to use graphic files for each digit displayed in the counter. You will need 10 files—`zero.gif`, `one.gif`, `two.gif`, and so on. When you output a counter number, use the proper graphic file for each digit (placing the numbers—that is, the appropriate graphic files—next to each other). For example, if the current page hit count was 34, you could output `three.gif` followed by `four.gif`.

7. Write a small product catalog application that allows the user to enter his or her name and select an item and a quantity to order. (Make up the three catalog items to display on the form.) When the user submits the form, append the user name, date, product to order, and quantity to a file and then display each order in the file (including the name, date, product, and quantity) in the new Web page. Notify the user of an error if an input field is empty.

CHAPTER SEVEN

MANAGING MULTIPLE-FORM APPLICATIONS

This chapter discusses how you can use PHP to create multiple-form Web sessions that can retain input data from one HTML form to another. The chapter describes three different ways to manage these Web sessions: *HTML hidden fields*, *browser cookies*, and *PHP session functions*. HTML hidden fields enable forms to pass data to form handling applications without displaying the particular HTML form element. Browser cookies allow Web applications to store data on a user's hard drive and are implemented by both Netscape Navigator and Internet Explorer. Finally, PHP session functions provide a convenient way for scripts to save user data and can be configured to retain the data using different methods.

◎◎ Chapter Objectives

☆ To understand what are multiple-form Web sessions

☆ To learn how to use hidden fields to build multiple-form user sessions

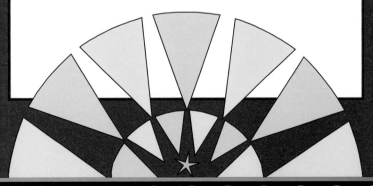

To learn how to use browser cookies to track data about the user

 To learn how to use PHP session functions and how to use them to track data about the user

 What Are Multiple-Form Web Sessions?

All the Web applications we have developed so far in this book have been only one or two screens long. Sometimes, however, you might need to write a Web application that presents a multiple-form Web session. A **multiple-form Web session** leads the user through a series of HTML forms that work together and pass data from form to form. A shopping cart and a multiple-page Web survey are two examples of Web sessions that may need to retain some data from screen to screen. As a small example, consider a Web survey with several forms that each ask two to three different survey questions. The survey might pass the user's name entered in the first form to each subsequent survey form that asks a survey question. This way the survey could customize each new survey form with the user's name.

As another example of a multiple-form Web session, consider an application that gathers product order information (Figure 7.1). This application has three screens.

1. *Order Info:* This form gathers a product code and a quantity to be ordered. When submitted, it sends the data to the *Billing Info* form.

2. *Billing Info:* This form gathers the customer's name and billing code. When submitted, it sends the product code and a quantity to order (from the first form) plus the customer's name and billing code (from the second form) to the *Save and Notify* form.

3. *Save and Notify:* This screen receives the product code, quantity to order, customer's name, and billing code and then saves all this data to a database or file. It also might send an e-mail to an order-handling department to notify them of a new order or to the user to acknowledge the order.

In this example, data that the user enters in the *Order Info* form is not saved to a file or database until the application gathers a complete order during the *Save and Notify* step. Some data will be passed to each screen using visible HTML form elements (such as the product code and quantity to order from the *Order Info* form). However, the *Billing Info* form also forwards the product and quantity received from the *Order Info* form to the *Save and Notify* form. Within HTML and PHP there are a few ways to manage such sessions and retain user data between forms. In this chapter we look at HTML hidden fields, browser cookies, and PHP session functions as methods for retaining user information.

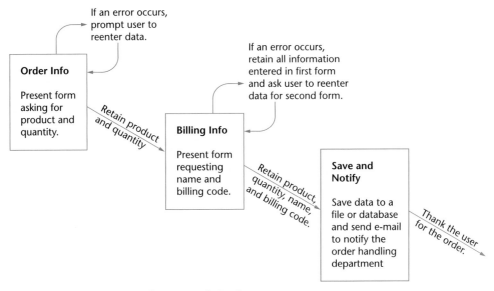

Figure 7.1 Example of a Multiple-Form Web Session

Using Hidden Fields

Hidden fields are not part of the PHP language. Instead they are HTML form elements that the browser does not display. Your scripts can use hidden fields to pass data values between HTML forms without displaying a form element. The receiving PHP script can retrieve any variable name and value defined in a hidden field form element like any other HTML form element.

Creating Hidden Fields

An HTML hidden field within an HTML form uses the general format shown in Figure 7.2.

> Specify a variable name to pass to the form processing script.

```
<input type="hidden" name="preference" value="Likes Power Tools">
```

> Set the variable's value to pass to the form processing script.

Figure 7.2 General Format of the HTML Hidden Field Form Element

☆**WARNING** **Hidden But Not Completely Invisible**

Hidden fields are hidden but not completely invisible to the user. In fact, a user can view them by looking at the HTML source (for example, by performing a `view->source` operation in Netscape Navigator or Microsoft Internet Explorer). For this reason, you shouldn't store any data in hidden fields that you don't want the user to be able to view.

The following example uses an HTML form and creates a hidden field. It provides a simplified version of the initial *Order Info* form used in Figure 7.1. This form looks like any other form to the user; that is, it is not obvious that it contains a hidden field. Note how line 7 creates a hidden field that contains a variable called `sample_hidden` with a value of `WELCOME!`. When the form-processing script at `http://webwizard.aw.com/~phppgm/C7/order2.php` starts, it can receive this variable's value just like any other HTML form variable. Figure 7.3 shows the output of the following HTML code.

```
1.  <html><head><title>Order Product</title></head><body>
2.  <form action="http://webwizard.aw.com/~phppgm/C7/order2.php"
                method="post">
3.  <font color="blue" size="5"> Happy Harry's Hardware Product
                Order Form</font>
4.  <br><font color="red" size="4">
5.  We have hammers, handsaws, and wrenches on special today!
6.  </font>
7.  <input type="hidden" name="sample_hidden" value="Welcome!">
8.  <br>Enter Item: <input text type="text" size="15"
                maxlength="20" name="product">
9.  Enter Quantity: <input text type="text" size="15"
                maxlength="20" name="quantity"><br>
10. <br><input type="submit" value="Click To Submit">
11. <input type = "reset" value="Reset">
12. </form></body></html>
```

Set `sample_hidden` in a hidden field.

Set `product` and `quantity` in visible HTML form elements.

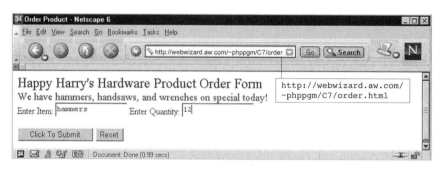

Figure 7.3 Order Info Form, Which Includes a Hidden Field

Here's a brief summary of the code above.

☆ Line 2 sets the `action` argument to start `http://webwizard.aw.com/~phppgm/C7/order2.php` when the user submits the form.

☆ Line 7 creates a hidden field that establishes a variable called `sample_hidden` with the value `Welcome!`. This variable's value will be available to the receiving script at `http://webwizard.aw.com/~phppgm/C7/order2.php`.

☆ Lines 8–9 create the visible text boxes for variables `product` and `quantity`.

Receiving Hidden Fields in Web Sessions

As previously mentioned, your scripts can receive variables set as hidden fields like any other data input from an HTML form. For example, when the user submits the *Order Info* form shown in Figure 7.3, the receiving script (stored at `http://webwizard.aw.com/~phppgm/C7/order2.php`) will have access to the value of `$sample_hidden` (set as a hidden field) as well as the values of `$product` and `$quantity` (set as visible form fields).

A multiple-screen Web session might use several hidden fields to retain data from form to form. For example, after the following script receives the data submitted in the *Order Info* form, it implements a version of the *Billing Info* form introduced in Figure 7.1. The script's output (Figure 7.4) shows the values of `$sample_hidden`, `$product`, and `$quantity` set from the *Order Info* form. The form also asks the user to input a customer name and billing code. When the user submits the *Billing Info* form, the script sends all the data to the next form in the session (that is, the *Save and Notify* form from Figure 7.1) through a combination of several hidden fields and visible form elements.

```
1.    <html><head><title> Order Product 2 </title> </head>
2.    <body>
3.    <form action="http://webwizard.aw.com/~phppgm/C7/order3.php"
                method="post">
4.    <?php
5.        print "<font size="5" color="blue">";
6.        print "Hidden value=$sample_hidden <br></font>";
7.        print "You selected product=$product and quantity=
                $quantity";
8.        print "<br><br><input type=\"hidden\" name=\"product\"
                value=\"$product\"> ";
9.        print "<input type=\"hidden\" name=\"quantity\"
                value=\"$quantity\">";
10.       print "<input type=\"hidden\" name=\"sample_hidden\"
                value=\"$sample_hidden\">";
11.       print 'Please enter your name:';
12.       print '<input type="text" size="15" maxlength="20"
                name="name">';
13.       print ' and billing code: (5 digits)';
14.       print '<input type="text" size="5" maxlength="5"
                name="code">';
15.       print '<br> <input type=submit value="Process Order">';
16.       print '<input type=reset>';
17.    ?></form></body></html>
```

Output `$sample_hidden` that was defined as a hidden field.

Set hidden fields for the next form.

Output visible HTML form elements.

Figure 7.4 Billing Info Form Output by a Script That Receives and Sets Hidden Fields

The following list briefly describes the script's key lines.

☆ Line 3 sets the HTML form tag to send the submitted data to `http://webwizard.aw.com/~phppgm/C7/order3.php`.

☆ Line 6 outputs the value of the variable `$sample_hidden` that was set as a hidden field in the *Order Info* form code. Its use here demonstrates how PHP scripts can receive variables set as hidden fields.

☆ Lines 8–10 set the values of `$product`, `$quantity`, and `$sample_hidden` as hidden fields so that these variables and values are available to the next script.

☆ Lines 12–14 generate the visible form elements that request the user to enter his or her name and billing code.

☆WARNING **Remember to Check for Input Errors**

Like other examples in this book, the multiple-form Web session shown in Figures 7.3 and 7.4 intentionally keeps the checking of form fields simple to minimize the script's complexity. For production applications you write, be sure your scripts carefully check and verify input such as billing codes, product names, and quantities.

Sending E-mail from a PHP Script

It is sometimes useful to send e-mail providing survey results, confirming order information, or notifying an order handler of a new order. For example, the *Save and Notify* form introduced in Figure 7.1 saves the form results and e-mails an order notification to an order handling department. PHP provides a function called `mail()` that by default sends e-mail via the Simple Mail Transfer Protocol (SMTP), which is a standard protocol for sending e-mail. The `mail()` function has the general format shown in Figure 7.5.

The `mail()` function accepts the following arguments.

☆ `to_address` specifies the destination e-mail address, that is, where the e-mail will be sent. For example, you could specify an address such as `harry@hardwareville.com`.

☆ `subject` specifies the subject of the e-mail. Set this argument to a string variable with the value you wish to use as the subject line of the message.

☆ `message` specifies the body of the e-mail.

☆ `extra_headers` identifies optional arguments you can use to set an *origination* address (`From:`) or a *carbon-copy address* (`Cc:`). To specify more than one header, you need to separate each argument with a `\n` character as shown below.

```
$extra='From: harry@harry.com \n Cc: orders@orders.com';
```

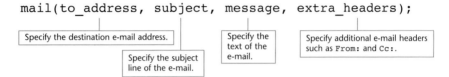

Figure 7.5 General Format of the `mail()` Function

The following PHP code segment shows the basic steps for using the `mail()` function to send e-mail. It creates a destination e-mail address (line 1), a subject line (line 2), the main text body (line 3), and then finally a `From:` line (line 4). Line 5 calls the `mail()` function to send the e-mail. Note how line 3 uses the new line character `\n` to create a new line (or carriage return) in the e-mail text.

```
1. $dest='orders@hardwareville.com';
2. $subject = 'New Hardware Order';
3. $message = 'Enclosed is a new order for 12 hammers.
   \n Thanks.';
4. $extra = 'From: harry@hardwareville.com';
5. mail( $dest, $subject, $message, $extra );
```

The PHP script below sends an order via e-mail to an order handling department at Happy Harry's Hardware. It implements a simplified version of the *Save and Notify* form introduced in Figure 7.1. This script (found at `http://webwizard.aw.com/~phppgm/C7/order3.php`) is called from the `order2.php` script from Figure 7.4. Note how it can access the values of the variables `$product`, `$quantity`, and `$sample_hidden` sent as hidden fields from the *Billing Info* form. Figure 7.6 shows the browser output of this script, and Figure 7.7 shows the e-mail it generates.

```
1.  <html><head><title>Order Product 3</title> </head><body>
2.  <?php
3.      $email='orders@hardwareville.com';
4.      $body = "New Order: Product=$product Number=$quantity
        Cust=$name Code=$code";
5.      print '<font size="4">';
```

Set the body of the e-mail message.

```
6.     print "<br>Sending e-mail to order handling department
           at $email ... </font>";
7.     print "<br>The e-mail body is <i>: $body. </i>";
8.     $from = 'harry@hardwareville.com';
9.     $subject = "New order from $name";
10.    mail($email, $subject, $body, "From: $from");
11.    print '<br><font color="blue"> E-mail sent. Thanks for
           ordering. </font>';
12.    print "<br>By the way, sample hidden=$sample_hidden";
13. ?></body></html>
```

> Send the e-mail message.

> The value of $sample_hidden is still available to this script.

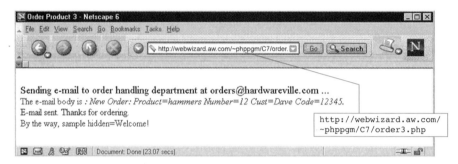

Figure 7.6 Save and Notify Form Output by a Script That Sends E-mail

Here's a summary of this script.

☆ Line 3 sets the destination address for the e-mail.

☆ Line 7 outputs a message to the user that includes the e-mail message text (in the variable $body). Note that the values of $product, $quantity, $name, and $code are received from the *Billing Info* script used in Figure 7.4.

☆ Line 10 calls the mail() function, setting the destination address, the subject line, the message body, and the From: address.

☆ Line 12 prints the value of $sample_hidden (originally set in the *Order Info* form shown in Figure 7.3) that has been passed along to this script. It is output here to demonstrate how a variable's value can be passed from form to form.

☆**TIP**   **Adjusting the PHP Configuration File**

On UNIX Web servers the mail() function often uses the sendmail utility to send e-mail. The sendmail program is preinstalled on most UNIX servers, but you may need to adjust the PHP configuration file (php.ini) to indicate where sendmail is installed (or to indicate the use of a different mail-sending program). Windows users may also need to set the location of a mail-sending program in php.ini. Another possibility is to redirect the mail() function to an e-mail server using options in the php.ini configuration file. Consult your Web server administrator or see the PHP online manual at http://www.php.net/mail for details.

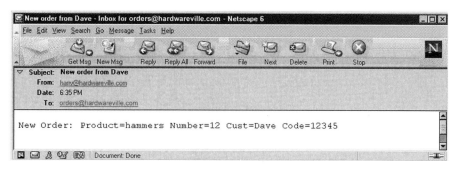

Figure 7.7 E-mail Sent by the Save and Notify Script

◎◎ Using Browser Cookies

Although Netscape developed cookies, today both Netscape Navigator and Microsoft Internet Explorer use cookies. Cookies are small pieces of data that a Web site application can save when a user visits the Web page. They are stored on the visitor's hard drive in a special "cookie" file. When the visitor returns to the Web site, a Web page script can read the previously stored browser cookie data and use it to "remember" something about the visitor.

☆WARNING You Are Probably Accepting Cookies Already

The default settings on the Navigator and Internet Explorer browsers are to accept all cookie data being sent. Thus, unless you disable this feature, your browser is likely set to allow cookie data to be stored on your hard drive.

As long as the user's browser supports the use of cookies and that feature is enabled, the Web page script can store any data it wants (with some size and volume restrictions). Cookies are typically used for tasks such as saving visitor preferences, managing sessions, and recording the frequency with which the user visits the site. For example, suppose you visit a site that sells books. While there, you fill out a form and indicate you prefer to read mystery novels. The site might then save a cookie on your hard drive that indicates you like mysteries. The next time you visit, a script on the site might read your cookie data and then suggest several mystery novels.

Understanding Cookie Limitations

Before learning how to set and read cookies, you should understand some of their limitations.

☆ *Users can easily disable the cookies feature.* Both Navigator and Internet Explorer provide methods for users to disable cookies and refuse to allow sites to set them. For example, in Navigator you can disable cookies by selecting *Edit, Preferences, Privacy and Security,* and *Cookies* and then changing the setting for cookie acceptance. (See Figure 7.8.)

☆ *People move around.* Cookies don't make much sense on multiple-user computers (such as those in libraries and computer labs). A cookie that stores a preference for one of the computer's users is not likely to be relevant for another user. Furthermore, people who visit a Web site from different computers (for example, at home, work, and school) probably have different cookie data sets.

☆ *Users may delete cookies.* Because cookie data are stored in one or more files on the user's computer, a user might accidentally or intentionally delete the data.

☆ *PHP sets a limit on cookies.* PHP limits the number of cookies per site to 20.

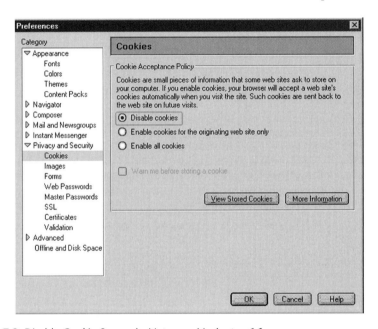

Figure 7.8 Disable Cookie Screen in Netscape Navigator 6.1

☆ **SHORTCUT View Your Own Cookie Data**

When you develop applications using cookies, you'll find it helpful to view the cookie data you create. In Navigator 6.1, select *Edit, Preferences, Privacy* and *Security*, and then *Cookies*. Next click the *View Stored Cookies* button on that screen (see Figure 7.8). For older versions of Navigator or Internet Explorer on a Windows PC, select *Start, Find, Files and Folders*, and then enter "cookie" in the search box. Navigator stores cookies in a file called `cookies.txt`. Internet Explorer stores them in a `cookies` directory.

Setting and Reading Cookies

Despite the limitations listed above, cookies are used extensively across the Web. Many sites use them to track user-browsing preferences. Some sites use cookies instead of hidden fields to retain data between forms. This section first discusses how to save a cookie and then describes how to read a previously set cookie.

Setting a Cookie

A Web application can request that a cookie be saved in memory or onto the user's hard drive. Cookies set in memory are deleted when the user exits from the browser. Those saved to the user's hard drive are retained (on disk) until some defined expiration date. With PHP you can request that the browser create a cookie by using the `setcookie()` function. Figure 7.9 shows the basic syntax for using `setcookie()` to create a cookie called `Customer_name` with the value `Denise` into memory from a PHP script.

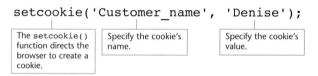

```
setcookie('Customer_name', 'Denise');
```

The `setcookie()` function directs the browser to create a cookie.

Specify the cookie's name.

Specify the cookie's value.

Figure 7.9 General Format for Setting a Memory-Only Cookie

The `setcookie()` function has a unique restriction: it must be run before anything else is output to the browser. (If you output anything else first, for example, a blank line or an HTML tag, the function will not work.) The cookie name is not a PHP variable name but a label for the cookie that the browser will use. You are free to set any string of characters (including numeric values) for the cookie name or value but you do not precede the cookie name with a dollar sign ($) like you do for PHP variable names.

When you want to save a cookie onto the user's hard disk, you need to specify an additional argument that sets an expiration time for the cookie. When that expiration time occurs on the user's machine, the browser will remove the cookie. A common way to set an expiration time for a cookie in PHP is to use the `time()` function. The `time()` function returns the current number of seconds since January 1, 1970. (That date is known as the UNIX epoch.) Thus the code shown in Figure 7.10 sets a cookie on the user's hard disk that will expire 10 days after the time it is set.

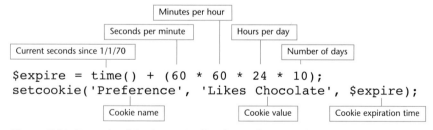

Minutes per hour

Seconds per minute

Hours per day

Current seconds since 1/1/70

Number of days

```
$expire = time() + (60 * 60 * 24 * 10);
setcookie('Preference', 'Likes Chocolate', $expire);
```

Cookie name

Cookie value

Cookie expiration time

Figure 7.10 Example of Setting a Cookie That Will Be Saved to Disk

The following example uses an initial input form to ask the user what items from Happy Harry's Hardware Catalog he or she would like to view. This initial input form (shown at the top of Figure 7.11) uses the following key HTML form elements to establish a text box (to set `custname`) and three radio buttons (to set `prefers`).

```
<input type="text" size="15" maxlength="20" name="custname">
<input type="radio" name="prefers" value="power tools"
                    checked > Power Tools?
<input type="radio" name="prefers"
                    value="hand tools"> Hand Tools?
<input type="radio" name="prefers"
                    value="air fresheners"> Air Fresheners?
```

When the user submits the form, the PHP script shown below runs, setting two cookies on the user's hard drive and then outputting some text back to the browser. The output appears in the bottom screen in Figure 7.11.

```
1.   <?php
2.       $expire = time() + (60 * 60 * 24 * 30);    ─── Set an expiration time for 30 days from when the script runs.
3.       setcookie("name", $custname, $expire);     ─┐ Set a cookie named name with the value of the $custname variable (input from calling form).
4.       setcookie("preference", $prefers, $expire);─┘
5.   ?>           Set a cookie named preference with the value of
6.   <html>       the $prefers variable (input from calling form).
7.   <head><title>Happy Harry's Hardware Catalog </title></head>
8.   <body><font size="4" color="blue">
9.   <?php
10.      print "Thanks $custname! ";
11.      print "Let's now look at $prefers... ";
12. ?> </font></body></html>
```

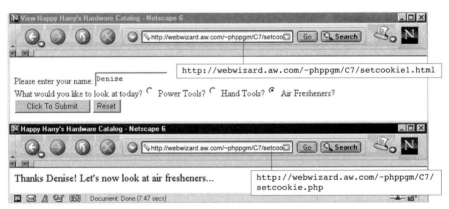

Figure 7.11 HTML Input Form (top) and Sample Output (bottom) of a Script That Saves Two Cookies to the User's Hard Drive

Here's a brief summary of the script.

☆ Line 2 sets the value of $expire to 30 days from the current time.

☆ Lines 3–4 set two cookies called name and preference using the values of $custname and $prefers (input from the calling form).

☆ Lines 6–12 output an HTML document. Lines 10 and 11 output the values of $custname and $prefers.

Reading Cookies

PHP makes reading a cookie from your script easy. Just use a PHP variable name with the same name as the cookie's name. For example, the following script reads the value of the cookie called `name` set in the script for Figure 7.11 using the PHP variable `$name`. It creates one message if the user has a cookie called `name` previously set (shown at the top of Figure 7.12 with blue text). It creates a different message, if the user has not visited the site before, or the cookie from the last visit has expired (shown at the bottom of Figure 7.12 with red text).

```
1.   <html>
2.   <head><title>Happy Harry's Hardware Catalog</title>
3.   </head><body>
4.   <?php
5.       print '<font color="blue" size="4">';
6.       if (isset($name)){
7.           print "Welcome back to our humble hardware site, $name.";
8.       } else {
9.           print '<font color="red">';
10.          print 'Welcome to our humble hardware site.</font>';
11.      }
12.      if ($preference == 'hand tools'){
13.          print '<br> We have hammers on sale for 5 dollars!';
14.      } elseif ($preference == 'power tools'){
15.          print '<br> We have power drills on sale for 25
                  dollars!';
16.      } elseif ($preference == 'air fresheners'){
17.          print '<br> We now carry extra-strength air
                  fresheners!';
18.      } else {
19.          print '<br> <font color="red">';
20.          print 'We have drills and hammers on special today!';
21.      }
22.  ?></font></html>
```

> Check whether the $name variable (set from a cookie) has a value.

> Check whether the $preference variable (set from a cookie) matches a tool name.

Let's briefly review the key lines of the script.

☆ Lines 6–11 use the `isset()` function to determine whether the `$name` variable has been previously set (presumably set as a cookie value). If `$name` has a value, it outputs a message using the value of `$name`. Otherwise, the code outputs a separate message without the value of `$name`.

☆ Lines 12–13 check whether the value of `$preference` is set to `hand tools` (presumably it was set as a cookie value). If so, the code outputs a special message regarding a sale on hammers.

☆ Lines 14–15 check whether the value of `$preference` is set to `power tools` (presumably it was set as a cookie value). If so, the code outputs a special message regarding a sale on power drills.

☆ Lines 16–17 check whether the value of `$preference` is set to `air fresheners` (presumably it was set as a cookie value). If so, the code outputs a special message regarding the availability of extra-strength air fresheners.

☆ Lines 18–20 output a separate message if `$preference` does not match `hand tools`, `power tools`, or `air fresheners`.

Figure 7.12 Sample Output of a Script That Reads Cookie Values

☆**TIP**   **Deleting Cookies**

Sometimes you may want to delete a cookie that you already set. You can delete a cookie by using the `setcookie()` function to set the expiration time to sometime in the past. For example, the following code sets a cookie named `preference` to a time in the past.

```
$expire = time() - 100;
setcookie('preference', 'Likes Chocolate', $expire);
```

Note that to delete a cookie you should use the same arguments you used to establish the cookie in the previous call to `setcookie()`.

☆**WARNING**   **Test Scripts Using Cookies Carefully**

Whenever you use cookies, be warned that different browsers and different browser versions may react differently. Be careful to test the script with each browser and each browser version that you expect visitors might use to access your site.

Using Browser Cookies

◎◎ Using PHP Sessions

Using the session_start() and session_register() Functions

So far, we have looked at hidden fields and cookies as ways to retain information from one Web page to another. PHP also provides a set of session functions that allow you to retain information between Web pages. These functions simplify the task of saving and retrieving session data. They also provide some additional functionality that using hidden variables or cookies alone doesn't offer. There are two key sessions functions.

1. `session_start()` either creates a new session or resumes one if a session exists. Run this function at the *start* of every PHP script that uses session data. If a session does not exist already, PHP will create a unique session ID for it. By default, this session ID is stored as a cookie, and then any session data is stored in a special directory on the Web server. If a session already exists, PHP will read the cookie with the session ID and then automatically make any previously saved session data values available to the PHP script.

2. `session_register()` registers one or more of the variables you specify as session variables. Once registered, their values will be available to subsequent PHP scripts in the session. Note that any variables you use with `session_register()` do not include the leading dollar sign ($) normal PHP variables use. The following PHP script segment shows an example of using `session_register()` to register two variables.

   ```
   $name = 'Matthew';
   $preference = 'Soccer Equipment';
   session_register('name', 'preference');
   ```

   Let's look at an example application that uses `session_start()` and `session_register()` to create a session and register some variables. The following script implements another version of the *Order Info* form (originally introduced in Figure 7.1) using PHP session functions. Note how line 1 uses `session_start()` to start a session. Also note how line 10 sets a value for `$sample_hidden` and then line 11 uses `session_register()` to register that value for `$sample_hidden`. The output of this script is shown at the top of Figure 7.13.

```
1.  <?php session_start(); ?> ──[ Start a PHP session ]
2.  <html><head><title>Order Product</title>
3.  </head><body>
4.  <form action="http://webwizard.aw.com/~phppgm/C7/
        sessions2order.php" method="post">
5.  <font color="blue" size="5"> Hardware Product Order Form </font>
6.  <br>We have hammers, handsaws, and wrenches.
7.  <br>Enter Item: <input text type="text" size="15"
        maxlength="20" name="product">
8.  Enter Quantity: <input text type="text" size="15"
        maxlength="20" name="quantity"><br>
```

```
9.  <?php
10.    $sample_hidden='Welcome Again!';
11.    session_register('sample_hidden');
12. ?>
13. <br><input type="submit" value="Click To Submit">
14. <input type = "reset" value = "Reset" >
15. </body></html>
```

Register the variable for the next session script.

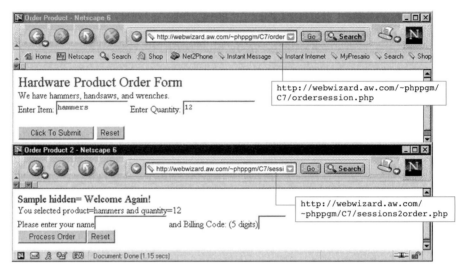

Figure 7.13 HTML Input Form That Starts a Session (top) and Sample Output (bottom) of a Web Application That Uses PHP Session Variables

Here's a brief summary of the key lines of the above script.

☆ Line 1 runs the `session_start()` function to begin a PHP session.

☆ Line 4 sets the action argument of the form to call `http://webwizard.aw.com/~phppgm/C7/sessions2order.php` when the user submits the form.

☆ Lines 7–8 create the visible HTML form elements that request values for `product` and `quantity`.

☆ Line 11 uses the `session_register()` function to register the value of `$sample_hidden`.

When the user submits the form shown in the top of Figure 7.13, this action starts another script at `http://webwizard.aw.com/~phppgm/C7/sessions2order.php` that implements another version of the *Billing Info* form introduced in Figure 7.1. Once this script (shown below) runs a `session_start()` function (in line 1), PHP makes the variable `$sample_hidden` available to it (line 6 outputs its value). The script also uses `session_register()` to make the values of `$product` and `$quantity` also available to subsequent scripts in the session. The bottom of Figure 7.13 shows a sample output of the following script.

Using PHP Sessions

```
1.  <?php session_start() ?>
2.  <html><head><title> Order Product 2 </title> </head>
3.  <body>
4.  <form action="http://webwizard.aw.com/~phppgm/C7/
        sessions3order.php " method="post">
5.  <?php
6.      print "<font color=\"blue\" size=\"4\">
            Sample hidden=$sample_hidden</font>";
7.      print "<br>You selected product=$product and
            quantity=$quantity";
8.      session_register('product', 'quantity');
9.      print '<br>Please enter your name';
10.     print '<input text type="text" size="15" maxlength="20"
            name="name">';
11.     print ' and Billing Code: (5 digits)';
12.     print '<input text type="text" size="5" maxlength="5"
            name="code">';
13.     print '<br> <input type=submit value="Process Order">';
14.     print '<input type=reset>';
15.     print '</form></body></html>';
16. ?>
```

> Output the value of $sample_hidden set as a session variable.

> Include $product and $quantity as session varibles.

The following list describes the key lines from the script.

☆ Line 1 uses the `session_start()` function to retrieve session variables saved for the current session.

☆ Line 4 sets the form's `action` argument to call `http://webwizard. aw.com/~phppgm/C7/sessions3order.php` when the user submits the form. This script would process the next screen in the session.

☆ Line 6 uses the variable `$sample_hidden` that was set as a session variable in the previous form.

☆ Line 8 calls `session_register()` to register the values of `$product` and `$quantity` as session variables. (Remember you don't precede a session variable name with a dollar sign.) These variables will be available to the next script (at `http://webwizard.aw.com/~phppgm/C7/ sessions3order.php`) when the user submits the form. Note that the script did not need to reregister the variable `$sample_hidden` since it was already registered.

☆**WARNING** Using `session_register()` within Function Definitions

The `session_register()` function makes variable values global in scope. It will not work inside a function definition unless the variables are defined as global inside the function. See the section on the `session_register()` function in the online manual for details (`http://www.php.net/ manual/ro/ref.session.php`).

Some Session Features

PHP supports some additional session features you can use to enhance your scripts.

The `session_is_registered()` Function

Use this function to determine whether a variable's value has been set from a session. This can be particularly useful when you want to ensure that the variable was not set as an argument on a URL line, such as, `http://mysite.com/order.php?name=George`. The function returns *true* if the variable was set from a session or *false* otherwise. For example, the following code checks whether `$name` was set from a session.

```
if (session_is_registered('name')){
    print "got name=$name from session";
} else {
    print "name=$name not set from session";
}
```

Session Configuration Options

You can define several session configuration options within the major PHP configuration file. This file is normally called `php.ini` on the Web server and is normally controlled by the server's Web master. Some configuration options include how long a session ID cookie will last (by default it lasts until the browser window closes), whether or not to use cookies to save session IDs (the default is to use cookies, but you can configure PHP to use the URL to pass session data), what directory path to use when saving session data on the Web server, and even what to name the cookie (`PHPSESSIONID` by default). See the PHP manual for details (`http://www.php.net/manual/en/ref.session.php`).

> ☆ **TIP** Destroying Your Session
>
> When you are done with your session variables and session ID, you can use two functions to clean up. The `session_unregister()` function unregisters each variable specified, so that each variable will no longer be a session variable. For example:
>
> `session_unregister('sample_hidden');`
>
> Use the `session_destroy()` function to destroy all data associated with a session and free up any session IDs used.

The `$_SESSION` Associative Array

You can also set and receive PHP session variables by using the `$_SESSION` associative array (for PHP version 4.1.0 and later; previous PHP versions use `$HTTP_SESSION_VARS`). Using `$_SESSION` has the advantages that you don't need to use `session_register()` to register the variable, and you don't need to use `session_is_registered()` to check whether variables accessed from `$_SESSION` are session variables. For example, the following code fragment uses `$_SESSION` to register the variable `$sample_hidden` as a session variable.

```
session_start();
$_SESSION['sample_hidden'] = 'Welcome!';
```

See the PHP manual for more details (`http://www.php.net/manual/en/ref.session.php`).

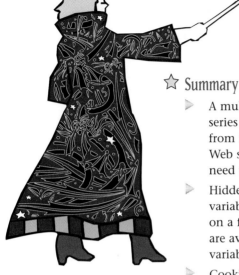

☆ Summary

> A multiple-form Web session leads the user through a series of HTML forms that work together and pass data from form to form. A shopping cart and a multiple-page Web survey are two examples of Web sessions that may need to retain some data from screen to screen.

> Hidden fields are HTML form fields you can use to set a variable name and variable value without displaying them on a form. The values of variables set as hidden fields are available to the receiving script like any other input variable.

> Cookies provide a way for Web server applications to store small pieces of data on the user's hard disk. Cookies can be refused or deleted by the user. Data set by cookies can be available for long periods of time, even when the user leaves the site and comes back later.

> PHP session functions provide a convenient way to retain data between PHP scripts. You can use the `session_start()` and `session_register()` functions to start sessions and define session variables, respectively. Use the `session_is_registered()` function to determine whether a variable's value has been set from a session.

☆ Online References

PHP online manual section that discusses sessions
`http://www.php.net/manual/en/ref.session.php`

Article that discusses user authentication, use of cookies, and session management in PHP
`http://hotwired.lycos.com/webmonkey/00/05/index2a.html?tw=programming`

Netscape's original cookie specification
`http://www.netscape.com/newsref/std/cookie_spec.html`

PHP Sessions Tutorial Information
`http://www.zend.com/zend/tut/session.php`

☆ Review Questions

1. What is a hidden field? How is it set?
2. What are the potential problems with using hidden fields?
3. What are the four arguments of the `mail()` function?

159

4. What is a browser cookie? What are three disadvantages of using such cookies?

5. Where are cookie data stored between times a user visits by a user?

6. What argument must you use to set a cookie that will be retained after the user leaves your site? What PHP function can you use to help set this argument?

7. Where does PHP session functions store data using a default PHP configuration?

8. What does the `session_register()` function do? Show the syntax of using `session_register()` to register the variables `$x` and `$y`.

9. Review the `sessions2order.php` script that creates the output shown at the bottom of Figure 7.13 and calls another script called `sessions3order.php`. What session variables will be available to the `sessions3order.php` script?

10. Using a default PHP configuration, how long are data registered with `session_register()` available?

☆ Hands-On Exercises

1. Create a Web survey that implements a three-form session. It should have the following pieces.

   a. On the first screen, ask the user's name and age. If the user fails to enter one of these answers, generate an error message and ask him or her to go back and reenter the input again. (Make sure the user's age is between 18 and 100.)

   b. On the second screen, ask two questions.
      1. Do you prefer to work with hammers or power drills?
      2. Do you prefer to do your own fix-it jobs or hire someone else?

   c. When the user submits the second form, summarize the results by displaying the user's name, age, and answers to the questions.

   Option 1: Use the `mail()` function to send the results to yourself.

   Option 2: Append the survey results to a file and then display all entries in this file to the browser.

2. Create a session application that implements a multiple-choice exam with the following four screens:

   a. An initial screen to collect a name
   b. A second screen that asks two multiple-choice questions
   c. A third screen that asks two more multiple-choice questions
   d. A final screen that summarizes the user's answers, scores the test, and thanks the user for participating

   Output the user's name on the second, third, and fourth screens. If the user makes an input error on a screen (like not filling in a field), notify the user and enable him or her to use the back button to reenter the data. Make answer **A** the correct answer for all the multiple-choice questions.

Option 1: E-mail the results to an e-mail address. Also save the results to a file and then display all entries in that file to the browser.

Option 2: Provide a password field on the first screen. (Make the password "secret00".)

3. Enhance the Web application from Figure 7.13 to implement a *Save and Notify* screen like the one introduced in Figure 7.1. (The example from Figure 7.13 currently implements *Order Info* and *Billing Info* forms only.) When the user submits the *Billing Info* form, have your *Save and Notify* script output all session data to the browser.

Option 1: E-mail the session information to an e-mail address.

Option 2: Save all order data to a file and then display *all* the entries in the file to the browser screen.

4. Create a form to allow a user to send feedback about your site. When the user enters feedback and submits the form, use `mail()` to mail the user's input to yourself. Format this information so you can easily read it when you receive the e-mail.

5. Create an HTML form that allows users to specify a preferred background color when visiting your Web site. Notify users that only red, yellow, green, and white can be used (and enforce that limitation). When the user selects a color, generate another screen that thanks the visitor. Set the background to that color (if a valid one was selected) and set a cookie with this preference. Write a script that ensures the background appears this color when the user visits your site again.

6. Create a "dice" guessing game. The initial form should ask the user's name, a guess of a die (from 1 to 6), and the number of points the user wants to bet (from 1 to 100). Give the user 100 points initially.

   a. When the user submits a guess and bet, generate a new form with a random number from 1 to 6. If that number matches the user's guess, add his or her bet to the point total. If the user guessed incorrectly, deduct the bet from the point total.
   b. Ask the user for another guess and bet.
   c. The game is over when the user's point total is 0.
   d. Do not let the user guess more than his or her remaining point total. If the user does guess more than this point total, generate an error message, remember the point total, and let the user guess again.
   e. If the user fails to fill out a field, notify him or her and allow the user to reenter data.

   Option: Use dice images (available on book Web site) for displaying the die roll results.

CHAPTER EIGHT

USING DATABASES WITH PHP SCRIPTS

Many Web sites provide information services such as product catalogs, driving directions, weather reports, and stock quotes. Often such information is stored in and retrieved from databases. This chapter explores how to use databases to store and retrieve data used in PHP scripts. It discusses the basics of using databases and then describes how to use a MySQL database to create tables, add data, search for specific data records, and change data.

Chapter Objectives

☆ To understand the advantages of using databases to store Web data

☆ To learn how to prepare a MySQL database for use with PHP

☆ To learn how to store data in a MySQL database

☆ To learn how to retrieve data from a MySQL database

☆ To learn how to update data in a MySQL database

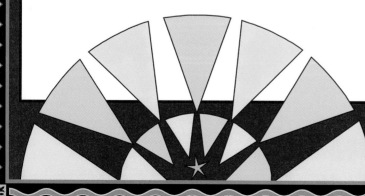

◎◎ Database Basics

A database is a set of data organized into one or more computer files. We essentially used a simple type of database in Chapter Six when we stored and retrieved data from files on a Web server. Using files works well when the amount of data to store is relatively small and the volume of concurrent access to the data is light. Sometimes, though, you need a more formal database system. Using a formal database system has some particular advantages over using files for storing data.

☆ *Faster access:* When a PHP script uses files for data storage and needs to search through the data, the script must read through the file one line at a time until it finds what it seeks. When data files are large, this sequential access can be slow. Database systems can generally search through large amounts of data much faster than scripts using data files.

☆ *Better concurrent access:* Since accessing data from a database system can be quicker than using files, Web applications that use databases can often handle more concurrent users than applications that use files for data storage.

☆ *Easier changes to data and scripts:* When a PHP script uses files to store and access data, it must know a lot about the data file format. If you change the format of the data (for example, add or delete new data fields such as customer name or product description field), several lines of the script might also need to change. Scripts that use a database access the data through a specially defined database query language, so changes in data elements usually have less of an effect on the PHP scripts that access the data.

☆ *Increased security:* When using files from a PHP script, the file access permissions must be set so that other users on the Web server can access the files. Database systems often use a separate user ID and password mechanism so that only scripts with the proper user ID and password can access the data.

Relational databases, the most popular type of database used today, store data in tables (usually more than one) with defined relationships between the tables. To keep things simple, let's look at a single product table that defines products sold by a hardware store. This table might contain a product number, product description, cost, weight, and inventory count for each product. In Figure 8.1 each row of the table defines a different product. You might decide that the product number is the unique identification field for each product row in the table. In relational database terms this unique table identification is called the **primary key**.

Product Number	Product	Cost	Weight	Number Available
0	Hammer	$5.00	12	123
1	Screwdriver	$3.00	2	144
2	Wrench	$2.00	1	150

Primary key →

Figure 8.1 A Simple Product Description Table

Choosing a Database System

PHP allows you to select from a wide variety of database systems, including Oracle, Access, Sybase, SQL Server, Postgresql, and MySQL. We will concentrate on using the MySQL database since it is the most popular database system used with PHP scripts. It is simple to use and provides enough functionality for many Web applications. It is also available for free download from its development site at `http://www.mysql.com`.

☆ **TIP**   **Using Other Database Types**

Using many of the other database systems is similar to using MySQL, but each database system uses different features and different PHP functions to access the database. For more information about other database systems, see the PHP Web site at `http://www.php.net`.

Using a Query Language

A database system provides methods to store, retrieve, and modify data. Many database systems (including MySQL) use a language called the Structured Query Language (SQL) to interface with the physical database. SQL is an old language developed by IBM to access databases on mainframe systems. It has since been adopted as an industry standard language for accessing databases. Figure 8.2 shows the interaction between a PHP script and a MySQL database. The figure illustrates that access to the data within the database requires sending SQL commands and receiving results back.

Figure 8.2 Interaction between a PHP Script and a MySQL Database

◎◎ Preparing a MySQL Database

Before you can store data in a MySQL database you need to get the database ready. You must first find a system with MySQL installed, then create a database, and finally create any tables that your application will use to store data. Let's look at how you can accomplish each of these steps below.

Installing MySQL

Probably the easiest way to start using MySQL is to find an ISP that already has it available for subscribers. Such ISPs not only have the database installed but usually also provide help in creating your own database instance (the next step described below). If you wish, you can install MySQL yourself on your computer and use it there. As previously mentioned, MySQL is an open source software project available for free download from `http://www.mysql.com`. This site also has excellent installation instructions that walk you through the installation process.

> ☆ **WARNING** **Running MySQL and PHP On Your Own Computer**
>
> Running both MySQL and PHP on your computer will work fine while you are learning to use the techniques described in this book. However, if you develop a production application that has external users and traffic, you'll probably want to move your application to an ISP that can offer higher throughput and availability for your application.

Creating a Database Instance

A single installation of MySQL can support several different databases being used by different applications and users. So before you can start to use a MySQL database from a PHP script, you first need a get a separate physical database instance created for your application. Usually database administrators create MySQL databases, but sometimes you can create an initial database yourself by using special control panel software or some other software interface. (You may need to check with your ISP or consult the online MySQL documentation at `http://www.mysql.com`.) Regardless, once you get a database created, you should receive a database name, a user ID, and a password. Make careful note of these items since you will need them later.

Creating Tables with SQL

Once you have an installed copy of MySQL and a database instance, you are ready to create database tables for your application to use. Since our examples use SQL commands to interface with the physical database, let's first examine the SQL statement you need to create MySQL tables. (We will discuss how to issue this command from PHP a little later in this chapter.)

You can use the SQL `CREATE TABLE` command to create your database tables. Figure 8.3 shows an example of an SQL statement that creates a simple two-column table, with the first column called `ProductID` and the second called

Product_desc. Notice that ProductID is defined as INT (to hold only numeric data) while Product_desc is defined as TEXT (to hold character data). Such data type definitions are required for each MySQL table column defined.

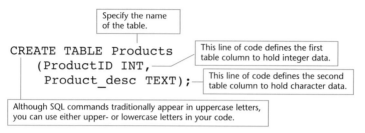

Figure 8.3 General Format of an SQL CREATE TABLE Command That Creates a Two-Column Table

MySQL supports several other data types (beyond INT and TEXT) that allow you to more precisely define the type of data a column can hold. When you create a table in a database, try to use the most efficient data type sizes possible to hold your data. (Efficiently using table space is especially important for large databases.) Here are a few of the data types supported in MySQL.

☆ TEXT specifies that the table column can hold a large amount of character data. Using this data type is simple, but it can use space inefficiently. The TEXT data type reserves space for up to 65,535 characters.

☆ CHAR(N) specifies a table column that holds a fixed length string of up to N characters (N must be less than 256). For example, CHAR(20) can hold a character string of up to 20 characters and if a string of only 12 characters is stored then 8 extra spaces are added.

☆ VARCAR(N) specifies a table column that holds a variable length string of up to N characters and removes any unused spaces on the end of the entry. For example, VARCHAR(20) can hold a character string of up to 20 characters. If a string of only 12 characters is stored then no extra spaces are added and any extra spaces at the end of the string are removed.

☆ INT specifies a table column that holds an integer with a value from about –2 billion to about 2 billion.

☆ INT UNSIGNED specifies a table column that holds an integer with a value from about 0 to about 4 billion.

☆ SMALLINT specifies a table column that holds an integer with a value from –32,768 to 32,767.

☆ SMALLINT UNSIGNED specifies a table column that holds an integer with a value from 0 to 65,535.

☆ DECIMAL(N,D) specifies a number that supports N total digits, of which D digits are to the right of the decimal point. (If you leave off the N and D then 10 total digits are assumed, with 0 digits to the right of the decimal point.)

A column's data type is just one column attribute you can specify when you create a table using SQL. Other column attributes further define MySQL table column characteristics. For example, Figure 8.4 shows an SQL `CREATE TABLE` command that specifies some additional table column attributes and creates the product description table shown in Figure 8.1.

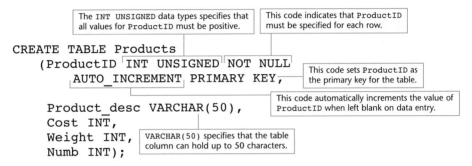

Figure 8.4 Format of the SQL Command Needed to Create the Product Description Table Shown in Figure 8.1

The `CREATE TABLE` command shown in Figure 8.4 creates a table called `Products` with five columns: `ProductID`, `Product_desc`, `Cost`, `Weight`, and `Numb`. Notice that each column has a defined data type of either `INT` or `VARCHAR`. In this example, the first column takes some additional arguments, listed below.

☆ `NOT NULL` indicates that the column must have a value.

☆ `AUTO_INCREMENT` can be used with integer columns to request MySQL to automatically increment the column's value when a row is added to the table with this column left blank on input. The value will be one greater than the column's largest value.

☆ `PRIMARY KEY` indicates that the column will be the primary key for the table (and therefore is a unique identifier). Only one column per table can be a primary key.

Issuing the CREATE TABLE Command from PHP

Now that you understand the `CREATE TABLE` SQL statement, let's look at how you can issue the SQL statement to MySQL. There are a couple of ways you can do this. If you have login privileges on the MySQL server machine, you can log in to the server and issue the needed SQL command to create the tables on the server (see Appendix C). If you don't have login access to the server, you can issue the necessary SQL command from a PHP script instead. Since this book assumes you do not have login access to the MySQL server, we describe how to create your initial tables using a PHP script.

To issue an SQL statement from a PHP script you need to connect to MySQL, select a specific database (remember that MySQL can support multiple physical databases simultaneously), and then issue an SQL statement. The following code segment uses the `mysql_connect()` PHP function to connect to a database, then `mysql_select_db()` to select a database, and then `mysql_query()` to issue an SQL statement to MySQL. Finally, `mysql_close()` closes the database connection.

```
1.  $connect = mysql_connect($server, $user, $pass);     ┐
2.  if ( !$connect ) {                          Connect to MySQL.
3.     die ("Cannot connect to $server using $user");
4.  } else {
5.     mysql_select_db('MyDatabaseName');
6.     $SQLcmd = 'CREATE TABLE Products(
           ProductID INT UNSIGNED NOT NULL
           AUTO_INCREMENT PRIMARY KEY,            Use the SQL
                                                  statement from
           Product_desc VARCHAR(50), Cost INT,    Figure 8.4.
           Weight INT, Numb INT )';
7.     mysql_query($SQLcmd, $connect);          Issue the SQL query
8.     mysql_close($connect);                   to the database.
9.  }
```

Let's review each part of the code segment carefully.

☆ Line 1 uses the `mysql_connect()` function to establish a connection to the MySQL server. You pass to it a host system (often localhost) your MySQL user ID and MySQL password. (You should have received these when your database was created.)

☆ Line 2 checks whether the `mysql_connect()` function was successful. If there is an error and the function returns *false*, the script in line 3 outputs a message and then ends.

☆ Line 5 uses `mysql_select_db()` to select a specific database to use. (You should have received a database name when your database was created.) Next, line 6 sets the PHP variable `$SQLcmd` to the same SQL CREATE TABLE statement shown in Figure 8.4. The `$SQLcmd` variable is used in the next statement in the `mysql_query()` function call.

☆ Line 7 calls `mysql_query()` to issue the SQL command to the database to create the table. The `mysql_query()` function accepts an SQL command to run (in `$SQLcmd`) and the database connection (saved in `$connect`) as arguments. If the `mysql_query()` function fails, it returns *false*; otherwise it returns *true*.

☆ Line 8 closes the connection to the database. If you inadvertently omit this command, the connection to the database is terminated when your script ends.

☆TIP   **Use of Semicolons with SQL Statements**

Note that SQL statements normally terminate with a semicolon. For example, if you use Telent to connect to your Web server and then log into MySQL and issue an SQL CREATE TABLE statement directly, you might enter the following line.

```
CREATE TABLE Products(Weight INT, Numb INT);
```

However, you omit the semicolon when you specify the SQL command from PHP (and thus use only one to end the PHP statement), as shown below.

```
$cmd = 'CREATE TABLE Products(Weight INT, Numb  INT)';
```

Let's now look at a complete example of a PHP script that connects to a database and creates an initial table. Such a script is generally used once to create the initial tables and then not used again unless additional tables are needed. Figure 8.5 shows the output of this script.

```
1.  <html><head><title>Create Table</title></head><body>
2.  <?php
3.      $server = 'localhost';
4.      $user = 'phppgm';
5.      $pass = 'mypasswd';
6.      $mydb  = 'mydatabase';
7.      $table_name = 'Products';
8.      $connect = mysql_connect($server, $user, $pass);
9.      if (!$connect) {
10.        die ("Cannot connect to $server using $user");
11.     } else {
12.         $SQLcmd = "CREATE TABLE $table_name (
                ProductID INT UNSIGNED NOT NULL
                AUTO_INCREMENT PRIMARY KEY,
                Product_desc VARCHAR(50),
                Cost INT, Weight INT, Numb INT)";
13.  mysql_select_db($mydb);
14.  if (mysql_query($SQLcmd, $connect)){
15.         print '<font size="4" color="blue" >Created Table';
16.         print "<i>$table_name</i> in database
                <i>$mydb</i><br></font>";
17.         print "<br>SQLcmd=$SQLcmd";
18.     } else {
19.         die ("Table Create Creation Failed SQLcmd=$SQLcmd");
20.     }
21.  mysql_close($connect);
22. }
23. ?></body></html>
```

Connect to MySQL. *(line 8)*

Define a CREATE TABLE SQL command. *(line 12)*

Select your database. *(line 13)*

Output a message if table creation is successful. *(lines 16–17)*

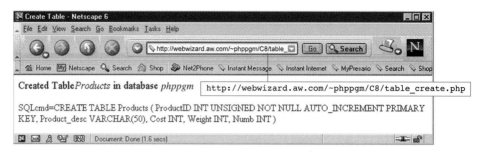

Figure 8.5 Output of a Script That Generates a Simple Initial Table

Here's a summary of the key lines from the above PHP script.

⭐ Lines 3–7 set the values of certain variables used in the script. Line 3 sets `$server` to the string `localhost` to indicate the name of the MySQL server to connect to. Next, lines 4 and 5 set `$user` and `$pass` to the MySQL user ID and password, respectively, defined when the database was created. Line 6 sets `$mydb` to hold the name of the database instance to use (also defined when the database was created). Finally, line 7 sets the string to use for `$table_name`.

⭐ Lines 8–10 call the `mysql_connect()` function to establish a connection to the MySQL server. The function sends the user ID, password, and database name as arguments. If the connection fails, the script outputs a message and ends.

⭐ Line 12 sets the value of `$SQLcmd` to the SQL command to run. It is the same command shown in Figure 8.4.

⭐ Line 13 calls the `mysql_select_db()` function to select a database to work with. Next line 14 uses `mysql_query()` to issue the SQL command defined in line 12 to the database. Lines 15–17 run when `mysql_query()` is *true*.

⭐ Line 19 runs when the `mysql_query()` function returns *false*, indicating the table creation was unsuccessful.

⭐ Line 21 runs the `mysql_close()` function to close the connection to the database.

⭐**TIP   Removing Tables**

You can use the SQL DROP TABLE command to remove a table from your MySQL database. For example, to drop a table, change line 12 of the script used to create the output shown in Figure 8.5 to

```
$SQLcmd = "DROP TABLE $table_name";
```

When you place the above line in your script (instead of line 12) and run it, it will delete the table defined in $table_name.

꩜ Inserting Data into a Database

After you have created your initial tables, you can insert data into them, including an initial seeding of data needed for your application (for example, entering your initial product inventory) and ongoing data additions (for example, adding new products or customers). To insert data into a database you use an SQL statement like the **CREATE TABLE** operation. The SQL statement shown in Figure 8.6 inserts a set of data into the table created in the script for Figure 8.5.

> Specify the name of the table into which you want to add data.

```
INSERT INTO Products VALUES
      ('0', 'Hammer', 5, 12, 123);
```

Each item goes into a separate table column in a table row.

Figure 8.6 General Format of an SQL INSERT Command That Adds Data to a Database

As before, you can issue the SQL INSERT statement from a PHP script. You first need to connect to the database (using `mysql_connect()`), select a database (using `mysql_select_db()`), and then issue an SQL INSERT statement (using `mysql_query()`).

The following example uses a PHP script to insert a row of data into the table we created in the script for Figure 8.5. This example uses the input form shown at the top of Figure 8.7 to get data values from the user. The form uses the following key HTML form elements.

```
Item Description: <input type="text" size="20"
                  maxlength="20" name="Item">
Weight: <input type="text" size="5"
                  maxlength="20" name="Weight">
Cost: <input type="text" size="5"
                  maxlength="20" name="Cost">
Number Available:<input type="text" size="5"
                  maxlength="20" name="Quantity">
```

When the user submits the form, it calls the following PHP script. Note how line 9 sets the SQL INSERT command and then line 13 issues the command to MySQL. The script's output appears at the bottom of Figure 8.7.

```
1.   <html><head><title>Insert Results</title></head><body>
2.   <?php
3.       $host = 'localhost';
4.       $user = 'phppgm';
5.       $passwd = 'mypasswd';
6.       $database = 'mydatabase';
7.       $connect = mysql_connect($host, $user, $passwd);
8.       $table_name = 'Products';
```

> Connect to the MySQL server.

```
9.       $query = "INSERT INTO $table_name VALUES
                  ('0','$Item','$Cost','$Weight','$Quantity')";
10.      print "The Query is <i>$query</i><br>";
11.      mysql_select_db($database);
12.      print '<br><font size="4" color="blue">';
13.      if (mysql_query($query, $connect)){
14.          print "Insert into $database was successful!</font>";
15.      } else {
16.          print "Insert into $database failed!</font>";
17. } mysql_close ($connect);
18. ?></body></html>
```

This SQL INSERT command uses input from the calling form.

Output this message when data was successfully added.

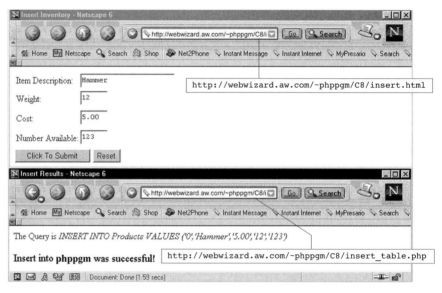

Figure 8.7 HTML Input Form (top) and Sample Output (bottom) of a Script That Inserts Data into a Database

Let's review the key lines of the PHP script.

☆ Lines 3–6 set values for the $host, $user, $passwd, and $database variables.

☆ Line 7 establishes a connection to the MySQL server.

☆ Line 9 sets a value for $query using an SQL INSERT statement and the variables $Item, $Cost, $Weight, and $Quantity, which receive their values from the calling HTML form.

☆ Lines 11–14 first use the mysql_select_db() function to select a database to use. Next the mysql_query() function issues the SQL statement to insert a row into the database. If mysql_query() is successful (that is, the function returns *true*), the script outputs a success message.

◎◎ Retrieving Data from a Database

Many Web applications allow you to search and retrieve data from a database. For example, a library patron may search a library database to display a list of all over-due books or to display the availability of a particular book. We examine two types of database search requests:

1. Retrieving all elements from a table
2. Searching for specific records in a table

Retrieving All Elements from a Table

Sometimes you may want your application to display all the elements in a table. For example, after inserting a new table row, you might want to display the entire table. Retrieving and displaying all the data from a database table is a two-step process: issue an SQL query command and then issue a second command to retrieve and display the query results. Let's look at each of these steps below.

Issuing an SQL Query Command

Use the `mysql_query()` function to issue a MySQL database query. The function does not actually retrieve the data but instead returns an *identifier* to the query results. You will later use that identifier to access the actual query results. The general format of an SQL command that outputs all the data from a MySQL table appears in Figure 8.8.

> Use the asterisk (*) to include all table columns in the query.

```
SELECT * FROM TableName;
```

> Specify the name of the table whose data you want to retrieve.

Figure 8.8 General Format of an SQL `SELECT` Statement That Outputs All Data from a Table

The following four lines shows how you can use the `mysql_query()` function to issue the SQL SELECT statement shown in Figure 8.8, saving the results into a variable called `$results_id`.

> Connect to MySQL server.

```
1. $connect = mysql_connect('Localhost', 'phppgm', 'mypasswd');
2. $SQLcmd = 'SELECT * FROM Products';
3. mysql_select_db('MyDatabase');
4. $results_id = mysql_query($SQLcmd, $connect);
```

> Select the database to use.
> Issue the SELECT SQL statement to the database.

The variable `$results_id` receives the output from the `mysql_query()` function call in line 4. In the next section you'll see how to use `$results_id` as an identifier to fetch the query results.

Retrieving the Results

Once you've used `mysql_query()` to query a database, you need to use the results identifier returned by the function to fetch the results. The `mysql_fetch_row()` function fetches the query results one row at a time. It uses the results identifier from the `mysql_query()` function as an argument and returns an array that holds one row of the query results.

As an example, the following PHP code segment uses the `$results_id` variable (set from the `mysql_query()` function call scripted in the previous subsection) as an argument to the `mysql_fetch_row()` function. The function appears within a `while` loop to incrementally retrieve each table row using the array `$row[]`. The code then uses a `foreach` loop to output each array item in `$row[]`.

> Access from the `mysql_query()` results in a different row for each iteration of the `while` loop.

> The `mysql_query()` function call sets the value of the `$results_id` variable.

```
while ($row = mysql_fetch_row($results_id)){
    foreach ($row as $field){
        print "Field=$field ";
    }
}
```

> Output each item of the `$row[]` array.

> Access each field in the table row results.

Combining the Steps

Now that you've seen how to use `mysql_fetch_row()` to retrieve `mysql_query()` query results, let's use both functions in one complete script. The following PHP script uses these functions to create the output shown in Figure 8.9, which displays the complete contents of the `Products` table (initially created in the script for Figure 8.5). The script outputs the results as an HTML table.

```
1.   <html><head><title>Table Output</title></head><body>
2.   <?php
3.       $host= 'localhost';
4.       $user = 'phppgm';
5.       $passwd = 'mypasswd';
6.       $database = 'phppgm';
7.       $connect = mysql_connect($host, $user, $passwd);
8.       $table_name = 'Products';
9.       print '<font size="5" color="blue">';
10.      print "$table_name Data</font><br>";
11.      $query = "SELECT * FROM $table_name";
12.      print "The query is <i>$query </i><br>";
13.      mysql_select_db($database);
14.      $results_id = mysql_query($query, $connect);
15.      if ($results_id) {
```

> Connect to the MySQL server.

> The SQL SELECT statement outputs the entire table.

```
16.          print '<table border=1>';
17.          print '<th>Num<th>Product<th>Cost<th>Weight
                <th>Count';
18.          while ($row = mysql_fetch_row($results_id)){
19.             print '<tr>';
20.             foreach ($row as $field) {
21.                 print "<td>$field</td> ";
22.             }
23.             print '</tr>';
24.          }
25.       } else { die ("Query=$query failed!"); }
26.    mysql_close($connect);
27.    ?> </table></body></html>
```

Fetch the query results one row at a time and output them as table cells.

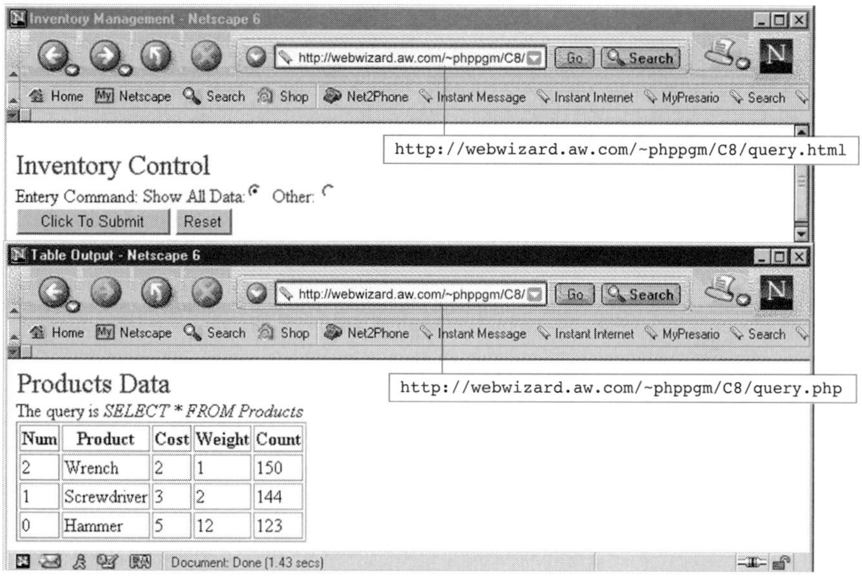

Figure 8.9 Results of a MySQL Query to Output an Entire Table

Here's a summary of the script's key lines.

☆ Lines 3–6 set the host name, user name, password, and database name for the MySQL database.

☆ Line 7 establishes a connection to the MySQL server.

☆ Lines 11–14 set an SQL query to access all data from the Products table and then use mysql_select_db() to select a database. Line 14 uses the mysql_query() function to issue the query to the database. The results identifier is saved into the $results_id variable.

☆ Lines 16–17 create the start of a table and output the table headers Num, Product, Cost, Weight, and Count.

⭐ Lines 18–24 use a while loop and the `mysql_fetch_row()` function to access a new row of the query results for each iteration of the while loop. The row output is stored in the `$row[]` array. A `foreach` loop accesses each item of the array and outputs it as a table cell.

⭐ Line 26 closes the connection to the MySQL server.

☆ **WARNING** **Check Return Values from MySQL Functions**

Make sure all your MySQL functions run correctly by looking for *false* returns from functions. For brevity purposes, the return values from all MySQL functions are not checked in the examples shown in this book. You can use the `mysql_error()` function to concisely access error results. It returns the text of any error message from the last MySQL command (or an empty string if no error occurred). For example, you can use the `mysql_error()` function as shown below.

```
$sql = 'SELECT * FROM tablename';
$result = mysql_query($sql) or die(mysql_error());
```

Searching for Specifc Records in a Table

Now that you understand how to retrieve all the data from a database table, let's look at using a database query that searches for specific records. For example, you might want to output all hardware items that cost more than a certain amount or output any item with less than three units left in inventory. A script that searches for specific records and displays the results is similar to the previous script that displays all elements in a table, but the search script uses a different SQL command format, as shown in Figure 8.10.

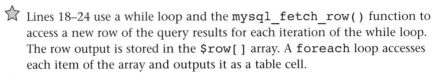

Figure 8.10 General Format of a SQL `SELECT` Command That Employs a `WHERE` Clause to Search for Specific Records

The SQL command shown in Figure 8.10 searches through all the records in the table called `TableName` and then evaluates `test_expression` in each table row. When `test_expression` is *true*, the script includes the table row in the query results. You can use several different test operators in your test expressions. Table 8.1 shows some common operators for SQL statements that use a `WHERE` clause.

The following example shows a PHP script that searches a hardware inventory database for a specific part name entered by the user. The top of Figure 8.11 shows the HTML form that requests the user to enter a product to search for in the inventory database. The form uses the following key HTML form element definition.

```
<input type="text" name="Search" size="20">
```

Retrieving Data from a Database

Table 8.1 Selected SQL WHERE Clause Operators

Operator	SQL Query Example	Meaning
=	`SELECT * FROM Products WHERE (Product_desc = 'Hammer');`	Retrieve those rows from the Products table that have a Product_desc column with a value **equal to** Hammer.
>	`SELECT * FROM Products WHERE (Cost > '5');`	Retrieve those rows from the Products table that have a Cost column with a value **greater than** 5.
<	`SELECT * FROM Products WHERE (Numb < '3');`	Retrieve those rows from the Products table that have a Numb column with a value **less than** 3.
<=	`SELECT * FROM Products WHERE (Cost <= '3');`	Retrieve those rows from the Products table that have a Cost column with a value **less than or equal to** 3.
>=	`SELECT * FROM Products WHERE (Weight >= '10');`	Retrieve those rows from the Products table that have a Weight column with a value **greater than or equal to** 10.

The receiving PHP script uses the user input (set in the `$Search` variable) to search the `Products` database. It creates an SQL query with a `WHERE` clause and then issues the query with the `mysql_query()` function. Finally a `while` loop iterates through the results from the query. The bottom of Figure 8.11 shows the output of the following script.

```
1.   <html><head><title>Search Results</title></head><body>
2.   <?php
3.       $host= 'localhost';
4.       $user = 'phppgm';
5.       $passwd = 'mypasswd';
6.       $database = 'phppgm';
7.       $connect = mysql_connect($host, $user, $passwd);
8.       $table_name = 'Products';
9.       print '<font size="5" color="blue">';
10.      print "$table_name Data</font><br>";
11.      $query = "SELECT * FROM $table_name WHERE
               (Product_desc = '$Search')";
12.      print "The query is <i>$query</i> <br>";
13.      mysql_select_db($database);
```

Use the SQL command to search the database.

Retrieving Data from a Database

```
14.     $results_id = mysql_query($query, $connect);
15.     if ($results_id) {                     Issue the SQL statement to the database.
16.         print '<br><table border=1>';
17.         print '<th>Num<th>Product<th>Cost<th>Weight
                <th>Count';
18.         while ($row = mysql_fetch_row($results_id)) {
19.             print '<tr>';
20.             foreach ($row as $field) {
21.                 print "<td>$field</td> ";
22.             }
23.             print '</tr>';
24.         }
25.     } else { die ("query=$query Failed");}
26.     mysql_close($connect);              Fetch and output the
27. ?> </body></html>                       results one row at a time.
```

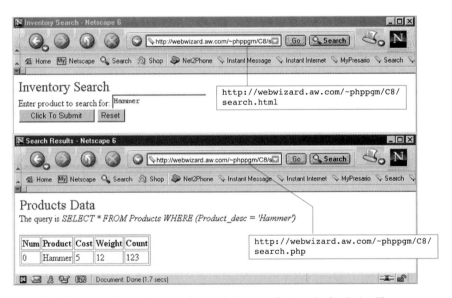

Figure 8.11 HTML Input Form (top) and Sample Output (bottom) of a Script That Searches a MySQL Database

Here's a brief review of the script.

☆ Lines 3–6 set the host name, user name, password, and database name for the MySQL database.

☆ Line 7 establishes a connection to the MySQL server and saves the connection information into `$connect`.

☆ Line 11 sets the variable `$query` to hold an SQL statement with a `WHERE` clause. The SQL statement looks for records with a value in `Product_desc` that matches the value of `$Search` (set from the calling HTML form).

☆ Line 13 uses the `mysql_select_db()` function to select a database. Line 14 uses `mysql_query()` to issue the SQL statement to the database. A pointer to the results is saved in the `$results_id` variable.

☆ Lines 16–24 begin the table and output the table headers `Num`, `Product`, `Cost`, `Weight`, and `Count`. The `mysql_fetch_row()` function in the `while` loop moves through the query and displays each row of the query results.

☆ **SHORTCUT   Deleting a Table Row**

You can use the SQL `DELETE` statement to delete one or more rows from a table. Use a `WHERE` clause to select specific table rows to delete. For example, the following statements issue an SQL command that deletes any row in the Products table with `Product_desc` equal to Hammer.

```
$query = 'DELETE FROM Products WHERE Product_desc = "Hammer"';
$Result = mysql_query($query, $connect);
```

◎◎ Updating a Database Record

Your Web applications will likely need the ability to update existing database records. A database update makes a change to fields within existing database table rows. Like other MySQL database operations presented here, you can use an SQL statement via the `mysql_query()` function to perform a table update. Figure 8.12 shows the general format of an SQL `UPDATE` command.

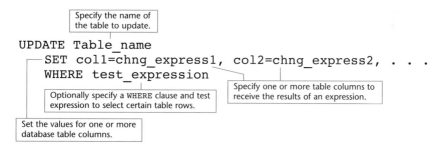

Figure 8.12 General Format of an SQL UPDATE Command

The SQL command shown in Figure 8.12 evaluates the `WHERE` clause's `test_expression` on each table row in `Table_name`. When `test_expression` is *true*, the script runs each expression defined in the `SET` clause affecting the specified column value. As an example, the following SQL statement looks through the `Products` table for values of `Product_desc` equal to `Hammer`. When it finds any such table row, it changes the value of the column labeled `Cost` to 2.

```
UPDATE Products
   SET Cost=2
   WHERE 'Product_desc=Hammer'
```

You can also use operators with your expressions in an SQL `SET` clause. Common operators include addition (+), subtraction (-), multiplication (*), and division (/). For example, the following SQL statement looks through the `Products` table for values of `Product_desc` equal to Hammer. When it finds any such record, it decrements the `Count` column value by 1.

```
UPDATE Products
    SET Count=Count-1
    WHERE 'Product_desc=Hammer'
```

★ **SHORTCUT Changing All Rows at Once**

If you omit the `WHERE` clause an SQL `UPDATE` statement operates on all rows in the table. For example, the following SQL statement sets the `Numb` column equal to 0 in all rows of the `Products` table.

```
UPDATE Products
SET Numb=0
```

The following example uses an SQL `UPDATE` statement to decrement an inventory count of an item in a table. An HTML form (shown at the top of Figure 8.13) asks the user to select a product and then calls the PHP script. It has the following key HTML form elements.

```
Hammer<input type="radio"
                  name="Product" value="Hammer">
Screwdriver <input type="radio"
                  name="Product" value="Screwdriver">
Wrench<input type="radio" name="Product"
                  value="Wrench">
```

When the user submits the form, it runs the following PHP script, which receives the selected product name (in the `$Product` variable). The script decrements the inventory count and then uses the `Show_all()` function (defined below) to display the new table values (see the bottom of Figure 8.13).

```
1.   <html><head><title>Product Update Results</title></head><body>
2.   <?php
3.       $host= 'localhost';
4.       $user = 'phppgm';
5.       $passwd = 'mypasswd';
6.       $database = 'phppgm';
7.       $connect = mysql_connect($host, $user, $passwd);
8.       $table_name = 'Products';
9.       print '<font size="5" color="blue">';
10.      print "Update Results for Table $table_name</font><br>\n";
11.      $query = "UPDATE $table_name
                    SET Numb = Numb-1
                    WHERE (Product_desc = '$Product')";
```

Decrement the value of the `Numb` column when the value of `Product_desc` is equal to the value of `$Product` received from the calling form.

```
12.     print "The query is <i> $query </i> <br><br>\n";
13.     mysql_select_db($database);
14.     $results_id = mysql_query($query, $connect);──┤ Issue the SQL query.
15.     if ($results_id){
16.         Show_all($connect, $database,$table_name);──┤ Call Show_all()
                                                          to output all data
17.     } else {                                          in the table.
18.         print "Update=$query failed";
19.     }
20.     mysql_close($connect);
21.     function Show_all($connect, $database, $table_name){
22.         $query = "SELECT * from $table_name";
23.         $results_id = mysql_query($query, $connect);
24.         print '<table border=1>';
25.         '<th> Num <th> Product<th> Cost <th> Weight <th>Count';
26.         while ($row = mysql_fetch_row($results_id)) {
27.             print '<tr>';
28.             foreach ($row as $field){
29.                 print "<td>$field</td> ";
30.             }
31.         print '</tr>';
32.     }
33. }
34. ?> </body></html>
```

The following summary describes the key lines from the above PHP script:.

☆ Lines 3–7 set the host name, user ID, password, and database name and then connect to the MySQL server.

☆ Line 11 creates an SQL command using SET and WHERE clauses. It decrements the value of the Numb column when Product_desc matches the value input from the HTML form.

☆ Lines 13–14 use mysql_select_db() to select a database and then mysql_query() to issue the SQL statement to the MySQL database.

☆ Lines 15–19 check the results of the mysql_query() function to see if the update was successful. If the function call was successful, line 16 calls the Show_all() function to output the entire Products table. If the function call was not successful, line 18 outputs a failure message to the user.

☆ Lines 21–33 define the Show_all() function. It issues an SQL SELECT statement to output all the rows of the Products table. It then uses a while loop and a foreach loop to output all the fields in each table row (similar to the script used for Figure 8.11).

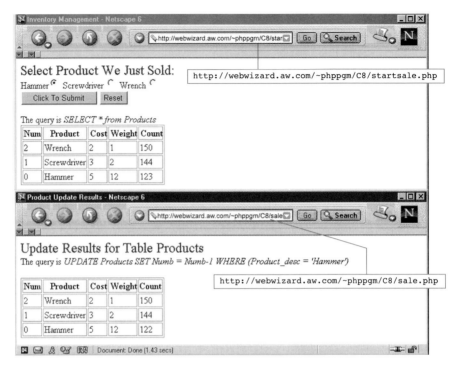

Figure 8.13 HTML Input Form (top) and Sample Output (bottom) of a Script That Decrements a Product Count

☆ **TIP**   **Placing Database Operations in Functions**

This example defines a function called Show_all() that outputs all rows of a table. It's common to place database operations in functions such as this so that other scripts can reuse them. This can really save time when you're developing database applications.

Updating a Database Record

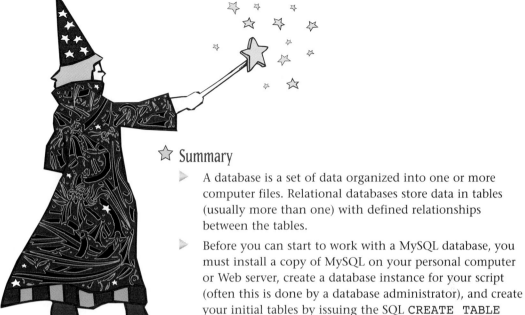

☆ Summary

> A database is a set of data organized into one or more computer files. Relational databases store data in tables (usually more than one) with defined relationships between the tables.

> Before you can start to work with a MySQL database, you must install a copy of MySQL on your personal computer or Web server, create a database instance for your script (often this is done by a database administrator), and create your initial tables by issuing the SQL `CREATE TABLE` command.

> Use the SQL `INSERT TABLE` command to insert data into a MySQL database. To issue the SQL `INSERT TABLE` command from a PHP script use `mysql_connect()` to connect to the MySQL server, then `mysql_select_db()` to select your database instance, and then finally `mysql_query()` to issue the SQL command.

> Use the SQL `SELECT` statement to retrieve data from a MySQL database and include a `WHERE` clause to select specific table rows. Use the `mysql_fetch_row()` function to gain access to query results one row at a time as an array.

> Use an SQL `UPDATE` statement to change records in a MySQL database. Include a `WHERE` clause to select specific table rows and a `SET` clause to define change expressions.

☆ Online References

Primary MySQL development site that includes downloads and manual
`http://www.mysql.com`

Online tutorial on SQL
`http://www.intermedia.net/support/sql/sqltut.shtm`

Online PHP and MySQL tutorial
`http://vtwebwizard.com/tutorials/mysql/`

☆ Review Questions

1. What are four advantages of using databases instead of files?
2. Name at least three different database systems that PHP can use.
3. What is a relational database? What is a primary key?

4. Show an SQL statement that creates a table called `Library` and has four columns: `title` (VARCHAR(50)), `author` (VARCHAR(50)), `isbn` (VARCHAR(30)), and `status` (INT). What PHP function would you use to create the table?

5. What does the `NOT NULL` argument define in an SQL statement that creates a table? What does the `AUTO_INCREMENT` argument define?

6. Show an SQL statement that enters the following data in the `Library` table described in Question 4: title="Cat in the Hat", author="Dr Seuss", isbn="12345-xx", and status="1". What PHP function would you use to issue the command to MySQL?

7. Show an SQL statement that outputs all books in the `Library` table (described in Question 4) that have `status` equal to 0.

8. Show an SQL statement that outputs all rows of the `Library` table (described in Question 4). What PHP function would you use to access each row of the results?

9. Show an SQL statement that changes a table row from the `Library` table (described in Question 4). Change any table row with Title="Cat in the Hat" to have `status` equal to 0.

10. Show an SQL statement that sets all the rows of the `Library` table (described in Question 4) to have `status` equal to 0.

☆ Hands-On Exercises

1. Create a customer database with a table called `customer_info` that has table columns for *last name* (VARCHAR(30)), *first name* (VARCHAR(30)), *e-mail address* (VARCHAR(50)), *preference* (VARCHAR(10)), and *total money spent on music* (INT). Create a front-end HTML form that enables you to enter the following data into the database.

Last Name	First Name	E-mail Address	Preference	Total Spent
Fuhzball	Jeremy	jfuhz@isp.com	Jazz	5.00
Flash	Matthew	mflash@isp.com	Rap	11.00
Davison	Mitch	mnish@isp.com	Jazz	22.00
Rams	Sean	srams@isp.com	Pop	122.00
Slick	Sam	sslick@slick.com	Pop	155.00

2. Create an HTML front-end form that enables the user to query the database table created in Exercise 1. Create a set of radio buttons that ask the user to select one of the following query types.

 a. Display all rows in the `customer_info` table.
 b. Display any row data that has a value in the `Total Spent` column of more than $100.
 c. Display all row data that has a value in the `Total Spent` column of $100 or less.

 When the user submits the form, query the database, and display the results in a table.

3. Create an HTML front-end form that enables the user to query the database table created in Exercise 1 for total dollars spent per type of music preference. Create a set of radio buttons that ask the user to select one of the following query types.

 a. Total all dollars spent on rap music.
 b. Total all dollars spent on jazz music.
 c. Total all dollars spent on pop music.
 d. Total all dollars spent on all music types.

 When the user submits the form, query the database, and display the results in a table.

4. Create a database table called inventory with columns for *item name* (`VAR-CHAR(30)`), *purchase cost* (`INT`), *sale price* (`INT`), *number sold* (`INT`), and the *number of each item in inventory* (`INT`). Create a front-end HTML form that enables you to enter the following data into the database table. After inputting each item, display all the rows in the table. *Hint:* Use the `Show_all()` function defined in the script for Figure 8.13.

Item Name	Purchase Cost	Sale Price	Number Sold	Number in Inventory
Hammer	5	12	122	26
Wrench	2	4	9	155
Screwdriver	3	5	55	115
Pliers	2	3	26	75
Handsaw	6	9	33	93

5. Create an HTML front-end form that enables the user to query the database table created in Exercise 4. Create a set of radio buttons that ask the user to select one of the following query types.

   a. Show the total profit and number sold for hammers.
   b. Show the total profit and number sold for wrenches.
   c. Show the total profit and number sold for pliers.
   d. Show the total profit and number sold for handsaws.
   e. Show the total value of all items in inventory (that is, the summation of the number in inventory times purchase cost for each item).

   When the user submits the form, query the database and display the results in a table.

6. Create a front-end form that simulates the sale of an item from the database table created in Exercise 4. When the user selects an item, decrement the number of that item remaining in the inventory and increment the number sold for that item. Redisplay all the items in inventory.

APPENDIX A: CONNECTING WITH TELNET

In Chapter One, we explained that you can use either Telnet or FTP to access your Web server and showed you how to connect to a Web server using FTP. This appendix discusses how to connect to your Web server using Telnet and introduces some basic UNIX commands you can use on a UNIX file server.

⊚⊚ Getting Connected

To connect to your Web server with Telnet, follow these steps.

1. Connect to the Internet if you are not already connected.

2. Start Telnet and connect to the server. Once you start Telnet you will see an initial Telnet screen. Use that screen to connect to your Web server. In Figure A.1, PuTTy is used to connect to a Web server called `dev04.ot.pearsontc.net`.

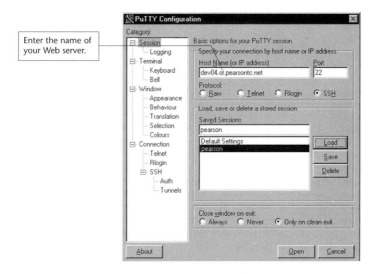

Figure A.1 Connecting to a Web Server via Telnet

3. If a connection is established, you will see an initial login prompt asking for your user ID and password (see the top of Figure A.2). Use that screen to enter your Web server user ID and password. Be careful when entering these since UNIX is case-sensitive. For example, the user ID `phppgm` is not the same as `PHPpgm`.

If you have correctly entered your user ID and password, the bottom of Figure A.2 shows the output you will receive. If you wish to end your session, enter the command `logout`.

Figure A.2 A Successful Telnet Login

◎◎ Navigating UNIX Directories

Once you connect with Telnet, you can navigate the directories on your UNIX file server with three basic UNIX commands.

Command	Command's Effect
pwd	Prints the working directory. Outputs the directory path of the current directory.
ls	Lists the files and directories in the current directory.
cd dir_name	Changes the current directory to the directory named `dir_name`. (Note that you can navigate up one directory by executing `cd ..` —that is, cd followed by two periods.)

Figure A.3 shows the output of using these three commands to navigate a Web server after logging in with Absolute Telnet. It shows the output of a `pwd` command, then `cd`, then `pwd`, and finally an `ls` command.

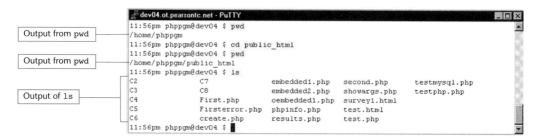

Figure A.3 Navigating a UNIX Web Server with Telnet

APPENDIX B: USING DATA FILES ON UNIX SYSTEMS

When you are using data files on a UNIX Web server, you should first ensure two things:

1. The location of the data files should not be in a place viewable over the Internet and
2. That you have properly set the permissions of the files

We discuss each of these issues below.

Choosing the Location of Your File on the Web Server

When your user account is initially created on the UNIX system, a home directory is also usually created in which you can store your files. All files and directories you store usually reside under your home directory. For example, in Figure B.1, the home directory for the user ID phppgm is /home/phppgm. From Figure B.1, you can see that jsmith has a home directory at /home/jsmith. Other directories, such as /bin, /usr, and /etc, are UNIX system directories that hold application programs, system programs, and files needed to run the UNIX system and Web server software.

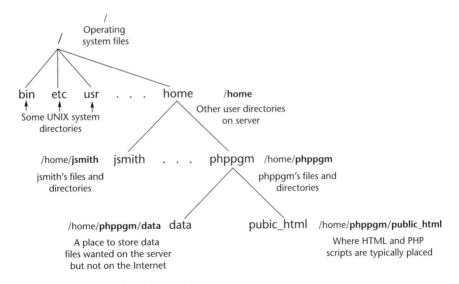

Figure B.1 High-Level UNIX Server Directories

Within your home directory you should store your data files in a directory not viewable over the Internet. For example, for the `phppgm` user ID, the data files are placed in the `/home/phppgm/data` directory. Placing your data in a nonpublic directory helps eliminate the possibility of a malicious user viewing (and possibly tampering with) data files to which he or she should not have access.

Setting File Permissions

A second item you need to ensure when working with UNIX data files is that the file access permissions are properly set. Here we review using Telnet and FTP to set UNIX file permissions.

Using Telnet

Using Telnet access, you can change your program's permissions by using the UNIX `chmod` command. Figure B.2 shows the use of the `chmod` command to change the access permissions of a data file to enable it to be read from and written to over the Internet.

Figure B.2 General Format of the UNIX `chmod` Command

As you can see in Figure B.2, you specify two things for the `chmod` command: a three-digit number and the name of a file.

The three-digit number really consists of three separate numbers. The first digit on the left sets your personal access permissions to the file—for example, read, write, or execute access permission. The second digit sets access permissions for your work group (usually your group includes only you, unless you define a group of users with whom you want to share your files). The final digit specifies the permissions for any other users on the system. Some possible settings for each of these digits are shown below.

Digit	Permissions Meaning
7	Gives read, write, and execute access to the file
6	Gives read and write access to the file but not execute access
5	Gives read and execute access to the file but not write access
4	Gives read access to the file but not write or execute access

The following examples illustrate some access permission settings for the UNIX chmod command.

☆ chmod 777 data.txt enables you, user IDs in your work group, and anyone else to read, write, and execute the file data.cgi.

☆ chmod 755 data1.txt means that you can read, write, and execute the file data1.txt, but everyone else can only read and execute it. This setting is useful for data input files.

Using FTP

Often on a UNIX Web server you can use FTP to connect to the server and change permissions to a file. To change permissions with FTP, connect to your Web server, navigate to the proper directory, and select the proper file. Next right-click the file and select chmod. Select the file permissions options in the *Remote file* permissions dialog box. Figure B.3 shows an FTP connection using WS_FTP_LE to a Web server with the file data.txt selected in the data directory.

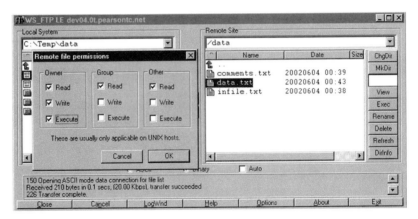

Figure B.3 Using FTP to Change Permissions on a File

APPENDIX C: EXECUTING SQL COMMANDS ON THE MYSQL SERVER

If you have Telent access to your UNIX MySQL server, you can run some of the SQL commands described in Chapter Eight directly on the server. This appendix shows you how to run the following tasks directly on a MySQL server:

☆ Connecting to the MySQL database

☆ Creating your initial tables

☆ Adding data to your database

Connecting to the MySQL Database

Once your administrator creates your initial MySQL database, you can log in to the system using the `mysql` command. If you use the —p switch, you will be prompted for your database password. For example, the following transcript shows a successful connection to a MySQL database.

```
mysql -p
Enter password: ******
Welcome to the MySQL monitor.  Commands end with ; or \g.
Your MySQL connection id is 298220 to server version:
3.23.21-beta-log

Type 'help' for help.
mysql>
```

If you entered an invalid password you would receive something similar to the following.

```
mysql -p
Enter password: *****
ERROR 1045: Access denied for user: 'phppgm@localhost'
(Using password: YES)
```

Creating Tables

Once you log in to MySQL, you need to connect to your particular database. (You should have received a database name when your database was created.) The following session connects to a database called **phppgm** (with the **use** command) and then uses a **show tables** command to show all the tables in the database.

```
mysql> use phppgm;
Reading table information for completion of table and
column names
You can turn off this feature to get a quicker startup
with -A

Database changed
mysql> show tables;
+------------------------+
| Tables_in_phppgm       |
+------------------------+
| Products               |
| Warehouse              |
| SurveyData             |
+------------------------+
3 rows in set (0.00 sec)
```

Once connected to your database, you can use a CREATE TABLE SQL command to create tables. For example, the following session creates a table called Customer.

```
mysql> CREATE TABLE Customer (ID INT UNSIGNED NOT NULL
->      AUTO_INCREMENT PRIMARY KEY,
->      Name TEXT,
->      Address TEXT);
Query OK, 0 rows affected (0.32 sec)
```

◎◎ Adding Data While in MySQL

You can use the INSERT SQL command to insert data into your table while logged into MySQL. This can be a handy way to quickly enter data into a database. For example, the following session shows an INSERT SQL statement followed by a SELECT SQL statement that shows all values in the table.

```
mysql> INSERT into Customer values( 0, 'Mr Smith', '1313
Monster Way');
Query OK, 1 row affected (0.01 sec)

mysql> SELECT * FROM Customer;
+----+----------+------------------+
| ID | Name     | Address          |
+----+----------+------------------+
|  1 | Mr Smith | 1313 Monster Way |
+----+----------+------------------+
1 row in set (0.00 sec)

mysql>
```

APPENDIX D: ANSWERS TO ODD-NUMBERED REVIEW QUESTIONS

◎◎ Chapter One

1. The acronym PHP originally stood for Personal Home Page; the name was later changed to PHP Hypertext Preprocessor. PHP was invented in 1994.

3. The advantages of PHP are that it is easy to use, it is an open source program, it works on multiple platforms, and it provides support for databases.

5. A Web server is a computer that stores files and makes them available over the Internet. It also runs special Web server software that enables it to respond to requests for Web pages.

7. A syntax error is a PHP statement that contains language errors. To repair such an error, reedit the script, correct the error, save the script, republish it, and then recheck it.

9. Script comments enable script developers to include descriptive text along with the script and are ignored when the script is executed. You can choose from the following characters to indicate comments: //, #, and /* ... */.

◎◎ Chapter Two

1. The invalid variable names are `$1st_counter` (first character after $ must be a letter or underscore character) and `squared` (variables must start with $).

3. Common numeric operators used in PHP include addition, subtraction, multiplication, division, and remainder. Common string functions include `strlen()`, `trim()`, `strtolower()`, `strtoupper()`, and `substr()`.

5. The output is Num `is 6 but x is 12`.

7. The output is `part=data part2=txt`.

9. The variable name is `$travel` with the value `Bike`.

◎◎ Chapter Three

1. Three types of conditional clauses are `if`, `elseif`, and `else`. The `if` statement can be used by itself.

3. You can use ==, <, >, <= and >= to compare string values using their ASCII code values. The `strcmp()` function also compares string variable values using the ASCII code values. The three possible output values are a positive number (if the first string is greater), a negative number (if the second string is greater), and zero (if the two strings are identical).

5. Two benefits of using loops is that scripts can be much more concise and also more flexible. Two types of loops discussed in this chapter are the `for` loop and the `while` loop.

7. The loop will repeat twice.

9. The output would be `ctr=6 ctr2=7ctr=7 ctr2=8ctr=8 ctr2=9 ctr=9 ctr2=10ctr=10 ctr2=11`.

◎◎ Chapter Four

1. The output would be `x=5 y=12`.

3. The output would be `numb=1, numb=2, numb=3`, or `numb=4`.

5. The output would be `y=24:2002`, where *24* is the two-digit number for the current day and *2002* is the four-digit number for the current year.

7. The following code defines the specified function.

```
function Output( $outvar ) {
    print "outvar=$outvar ";
}
```

9. Arguments are input variables sent to a function. The following is a call to the `Calc_perc()` function that would enable the function to change the value of `$buy`.

```
Calc_perc( &$buy, $sell);
```

◎◎ Chapter Five

1. Three advantages of using arrays are the abilities to include a flexible number of array items, to examine each item more concisely, and to use special array operators and functions.

3. The following `print` statement outputs the array in reverse order.

```
print "$list1[3], $list1[2], $list1[1], $list1[0]";
```

5. The output is `sublist=7 5`.

7. The values of `$x`, `$y`, and `$z` are 31, 62, and 3, respectively.

9. The `unset()` function destroys the specified variable. The `isset()` function verifies whether a particular index exists.

Chapter Six

1. This statement checks whether the value of `$name` contains the sequence "ABC".

   ```
   if (ereg('ABC', $name)){
   ```

   This statement checks whether the value of `$name` contains either "ABC" or "DEF".

   ```
   if (ereg('(ABC)|(DEF)', $name)){
   ```

3. Two examples of values for `$name` that make the test condition *true* are "AA11" and "CA92 is OK". An example of a value that makes it *false* is "92CA".

5. ^   Matches when the following character starts the string

   $ Matches when the preceding character ends the string

   +   Matches when the string contains one or more occurrences of the preceding character

   *   Matches when the string contains zero or more occurrences of the preceding character

   .   Indicates a wildcard symbol that matches any one character

   | Indicates an alternation symbol that matches either character pattern specified

7. The script outputs "12.50 22".

9. The six modes are read-only mode, read and write mode, write-only mode, read and write overwrite mode, append mode, and read and append mode.

11. The `rewind()` function resets the file pointer to the start of the file.

Chapter Seven

1. A hidden field is an HTML form element that is not visible on the form. The following is an example of the syntax used to set a hidden field.

   ```
   <input type="hidden" name="Name" value="Harry">
   ```

3. The `mail()` function takes arguments for the destination address, the subject, the e-mail text, and extra e-mail headers.

5. Cookie data are stored on the hard drive of the visiting user's machine.

7. In a default configuration, PHP session functions create a session ID as a cookie and store session data in a file on the Web server.

9. The session variables available would be `$product`, `$quantity`, and `$sample_hidden`.

◎◎ Chapter Eight

1. Four advantages of using databases instead of files are faster access, better concurrent access, the use of an independent data access language, and increased security.

3. A relational database stores data into one or more tables with defined relationships between tables. A primary key is a unique identification field for each row in a table.

5. The `NOT NULL` argument indicates that the column's variable must be specified and cannot be omitted when a new table row is added. The `AUTO_INCREMENT` argument requests that the system automatically increment its value for each row added to the table.

7. The following SQL statement outputs all books in the `Library` table that have `status` equal to 0.

   `SELECT * FROM Library WHERE status=0`

9. The following SQL statement sets `status` to 0 for all rows in the `Library` table that have `title` equal to `Cat in the Hat`.

   `UPDATE Library SET status=0 WHERE Title="Cat in the Hat"`

INDEX

Symbols

" (quotation marks), PHP syntax, 10
; (semicolon)
    for loops and, 51
    PHP syntax and, 10, 19
    SQL statements and, 169
– (subtraction) operator, 21
! (NOT) operator, 55
!= (not equal to), 41
&& (AND) operator, 55
$ (dollar) symbol
    pattern-matching, 113
    variable names and, 19
$_SESSION associative array, 158
% (remainder) operator, 21
( ) (parentheses)
    character group specification, 115–116
    operator precedence, 24
    PHP syntax and, 10
    test expressions and, 40
* (multiplication) operator, 21
* (asterisk) symbol, pattern-matching, 113
. (period) symbol, pattern-matching, 113
/ (division) operator, 21
// (forward slashes), 13
: (colon), field separation, 131
?: (tenary operator), 49
[ ] (square brackets), 115, 116–117
[[:alpha:]], special character classes, 118
[[:digit:]], special character classes, 118
[[:lower:]], special character classes, 118
[[:punct:]], special character classes, 118
[[:space:]], special character classes, 118
[[:upper:]], special character classes, 118
\ (backslash)
    HTML tags and, 12
    PHP syntax and, 10
\n character (new line), 12, 132
^ (caret) symbol, pattern-matching, 113, 117
_ (underscore character), 19

{ } (curly brackets)
    character group specification, 115–116
    test expressions and, 40
|| (OR) operator, 55
| (pipe) symbol, pattern-matching, 113
+ (addition) operator, 21
+ (plus) symbol, pattern-matching, 113
< (less than), 41
<= (less than or equal to), 41
= (equal sign), assignment operator, 40
== (equal signs), testing equal values, 40, 41
> (greater than), 41
>= (greater than or equal to), 41

A

a (append) mode, 126, 130, 133
a+ (read and append) mode, 126
abs( ) function, 62
addition (+) operator, 21
American Standard Code for Information Interchange (ASCII), 43
AND operator (&&), 55
Apache Software Foundation, 3
Apache Web Sever, 5
append (a) mode, 126, 130, 133
arguments
    AUTO_INCREMENT argument, 167
    changing values of, 76–79
    ereg( ) function, 111–112
    filename argument, 126
    NOT NULL argument, 167
    optional, 76
    passing to functions, 72–74
    PRIMARY KEY argument, 167
    sending correct number of, 73
arguments to the function, 72
arithmetic operators, 21–24
    automatic increment/decrement operators, 23

◎◎ Selected PHP Functions Used in Book

String Functions

Function	Effect
`$r = ereg("pattern", $str1);`	Returns *true* if `"pattern"` (that may include regular expressions) is found in the string `$str1`.
`$newstr = ereg_replace("pattern", $repl, $str1);`	Searches for `"pattern"` (that may include regular expressions) in the string `$str1` and replaces any matches with the string `$repl`. The changed string is placed into `$newstr`.
`$outlist = split("pattern",$str1, $max);`	Splits the string `$str1` into `$outlist` array using `"pattern"` (that may include regular expressions) as a field delimiter. If specified, no more than `$max` number of matches are made.
`$ret = strcmp($str1, $str2);`	Compares string `$str1` with string `$str2` and returns to `$ret` a *positive* number if `$str1` is greater than `$str2`, A *negative* number if `$str1` is less than `$str2`, or *zero* if the two strings are identical.
`$len = strlen($str1);`	Returns the number of characters in the string `$str1` to `$len`.
`$lower = strtolower($str1);`	Returns the string `$str1` in all lower cases to `$lower`.
`$upper = strtoupper($str1);`	Returns the string `$str1` in all upper cases to `$upper`.
`$new = substr($str1, $n1, $n2)`	Returns a sub-string of string `$str1` from position number `$n1` to number `$n2` to `$new`.
`$str2 = trim($str1);`	Returns into `$str2` the string `$str1` with leading and trailing spaces removed.

Numeric, Time, and Mail Functions

Function	Effect
`$y = abs($x);`	Returns to `$y` the absolute value of `$x`.
`$ret = is_numeric($input);`	Sets `$ret` to *true* if `$input` is a number or numeric string.
`$ret = is_null($x);`	Returns *true* to `$ret` if `$x` is has a NULL value.
`$ret = mail($to_addr, $subject, $msg, $ex_hdr);`	Sends email to the `$to_addr` with subject `$subject`, and email body `$msg`. The string `$ex_hdrs` optionally sets extra headers, for example copy to " Cc:". Returns *true* if message successfully sent and *false* otherwise.
`$x=round($num,2);`	Returns to `$x` the value of `$num` rounded to 2 decimal places.

(continues)

Numeric, Time, and Mail Functions *(continued)*

Function	Effect
`srand( (double)microtime()*10000000); $dice = rand(1, 6);`	Generates a random number from 1, 2, 3, ... 6 into `$dice`.
`$ret = time();`	Returns into `$ret` the number of seconds since January 1 1970 00:00:00 GMT.

File, Cookie, and Session Functions

Function	Effect
`$var = fgets($fileh, $len);`	Reads from the file handle `$fileh`. Returns into `$var` either a string of up to `$len` −1 bytes read or *false* (if error). If you are using PHP version 4.2.0 or later, then you do not need to specify the length parameter.
`$r = flock($fileh, LOCK_EX);`	Acquires an exclusive lock for access to the file that `$fileh` points to. (Returns *true* if successful and *false* otherwise.)
`$fileh = fopen($fileloc, 'mode');`	Opens the file at file path `$fileloc` for the specified file open mode, returns a file handle to `$fileh` (or *false* if error). The file open modes are read-only mode (`'r'`), read and write mode (`'r+'`) that starts with the file pointer at the beginning of the file, write-only mode (`'w'`), read and write mode (`'w+'`) that starts with the file pointer at the beginning of the file but overwrites the file if it exists, append mode (`'a'`), and read and write mode (`'a+'`) that starts with the file pointer at the end of the file.
`$r = fputs($fileh, $msg);`	Writes the value of `$msg` into the file that file handle `$fileh` points to. Returns *false* if error and *true* otherwise.
`$r = rewind($fileh);`	Reset the file pointer to the file indicated by the file handle `$fileh` to the start of the file.
`$ret = session_is_registered ('v_name');`	Returns *true* if the variable named `'v_name'` is a registered variable in the current session.
`session_start();`	Either starts a session or resumes if one exists. If one exists it makes any session variables available to the calling script. It must be called before anything is output to the browser when you use cookie-based sessions.
`session_register('var_name');`	Registers the variable name `'var_name'` as a session variable.
`setcookie ('Cname','Cval', $exp);`	Sends a cookie to the browser with name cookie name `'Cname'` and cookie value `'Cval'` that will expire at in `$exp` seconds. It must be called before anything is output to the browser.